The Basic Basics
MICROWAVE COOKING FOR ONE & TWO

GW00470759

Carol Bowen Ball

GRUB STREET • LONDON

For Peter

And for his amazing ability and capability to even now taste, scrutinise and comment on sweet before savoury and then back again, or sample pudding before starter several times daily when a book is 'cooking'. It's always been a joint effort ….

Published in 2023 by
Grub Street
4 Rainham Close
London
SW11 6SS

Email: food@grubstreet.co.uk
Web: www.grubstreet.co.uk
Twitter: @grub_street
Facebook: Grub Street Publishing
Instagram: @grubstreet_books

A CIP catalogue record for this book is available from the British Library

ISBN 978-1-911667-47-6

Design by Myriam Bell Design, UK
Printed and bound by Finidr, Czech Republic

CONTENTS

STARTERS AND LIGHT MEALS

SNACKS

MAIN MEALS   64

FISH

MEAT

POULTRY

DRESSINGS

DESSERTS   164

INDEX   191

PREFACE

I've long been an admirer and advocate for the under-rated cooking 'wonder box' – aka the microwave, even throughout its chequered history of initial highs, and then subsequent lows, charted over many years.

After a heady start in the 80s (when perhaps it over-promised so much) it then suffered some depressing lows when no self-respecting celebrity chef, gourmet cook or foodie would admit to owning one, never mind cooking in one. And then along came the once-in-a-generation cost-of-living and energy fuel crisis and cooks everywhere have had a massive rethink about the bleeping box in the kitchen that defrosts, cooks and reheats food in 90% of homes – cheaply and fast!

This crisis has thrown the microwave into the spotlight again as a star performer mainly because it's one of the most energy efficient and thrifty ways of cooking food. Yes, it even knocks slow cookers, pressure cookers and air fryers down the ratings to take top spot.

I've smiled a good deal recently at such conversions because, despite the haters, the microwave has remained a firm fixture in my own kitchen for over 30 years, and I use it virtually every day. I'm more than a convert – I would even admit to, and not ashamed of saying, I have something of a long-standing love affair with mine. I don't just love the money-saving aspect of it but the way it makes such light work of meal preparation – and I think I have, after all this time, got a good perspective on what it's ideal for and what it's not.

The microwave is just one of the appliances I use in my kitchen but one I would be more than loathe to lose. But it is a loyal adjunct to my conventional oven, grill, food processor, toaster, refrigerator and freezer and any number of other modern cooking machines that cook and store food, it's not a total replacement for any and justly earns its valuable and necessary place. I like to use any number of them in tandem with each other to get the best results without compromising on taste, time or value for money. So you'll find that sometimes I start my casseroles and stews in the microwave and then finish in the slow cooker or conventional oven (I still save massively on cooking time and energy but don't sacrifice on flavour). I tend to always cook side-dish vegetables in the microwave rather than on the hob (because they cook to just-tender perfection), but might finish a microwave cooked gratin style quick cook meal with a quick zap under the grill to get a golden and crisp crown before serving.

If there is one over-riding benefit I have found over time it's that the microwave comes into its own when cooking smaller quantities. The accolades flood in and are numerous when cooking for one or two portions. Maybe 'working from home (WFH)' diners have driven this popularity up – but a quick microwave meal mid-way through the working day can beat hands down a supermarket sandwich, pre-packaged ready-meal or some hurried 'food on the run'. And cooking from home can be cheaper too.

This latest recipe collection of mine still has many of my time-honoured choices but some newly developed favourites too – they have been enjoyed when I cook for my husband and myself, when I cater for a friend at lunchtime, many times when I eat alone and then again when I cook for the pure pleasure of it. I hope you will enjoy my selection and that they may become some of your favourites too.

INTRODUCTION

What are microwaves?

The chances are if you are a freezer-owner or busy cook, you will have welcomed the arrival of the microwave oven. For with a microwave to help, you will be able to cook speedily, defrost and reheat food in seconds instead of the usual minutes or hours of conventional cooking. But what are microwaves and where do they come from?

The mechanics of the microwave oven are no more magical than a television or radio. Inside the microwave is a magnetron vacuum tube – this is the 'heart' of the microwave and converts ordinary household electrical energy into high frequency electro-magnetic waves, called microwaves. Once produced, the microwaves are then directed into the oven cavity, through a wave guide and stirred, by a fan, for even distribution.

These waves are then either reflected, pass through or are absorbed by different materials. Metals reflect them (so cooking utensils must be non-metallic), glass, pottery, paper and most plastics allow them to pass through (which is why they make ideal cooking utensils) and foods absorb them. The microwaves are absorbed by the moisture in food, causing the food molecules to vibrate rapidly, thus producing heat to cook food. The speed at which microwaves cause the molecules to vibrate is millions of times per second – producing an intense heat that cooks extra fast.

It is a completely different method of cooking food compared with conventional methods – especially since dishes remain cool, metals cannot be used and timings are extra speedy... and as a result different cooking procedures and techniques are called into action.

The microwave cooker

All basic models are pretty much the same in design. They consist of a cabinet, magnetron, wave guide, wave stirrer, power supply, power cord and controls. Some have special extra features like automatic defrost, variable power control, turntable, integral thermometer or temperature probe and browning or crisping elements. Varying only slightly in design, they all work in the same way – microwaves are produced in the magnetron and are passed into the oven cavity through the wave guide to be stirred by a fan. Once there, the microwaves are safely contained in the cavity since the base and walls are made of metal and deflect the microwaves into the food. All cooker doors and frames are fitted with special seals as an extra safety measure to ensure microwaves stay in the cooker. In addition, all microwave cookers have one or more cut-out devices so that the flow of microwaves stops automatically whenever the door is opened or indeed if the door has not been shut properly.

Within the vast selection of microwave ovens available three basic models can be identified:

Portable microwave ovens

At the present time these are still the most popular ovens on the market. Almost as light and portable as a TV they simply require a 13- or 15-amp plug for use and will happily sit on a convenient work surface, trolley or other firm, stable surface for operation.

Double oven cooker

A few microwave models are available teamed up, and in the same unit as a conventional cooker – here the microwave acts as a second or double oven. Most are built-in but a few are available free-standing.

Combination cooker

Deemed to be the fastest growing sector of the microwave oven market and certainly worthy of interest, these ovens have the facility to cook by both microwave and conventionally in one operation and in one unit – also in tandem or sequence with each other. Some models offer further choices with fan assistance, grilling and automatic roasting controls linked with the microwave. Latest models also come with steam cooking – via a refillable water reservoir. Many also have special programmes that you can pre-set to take away much of the guesswork of timings. Many are simple and helpful but like a washing machine that has 12 programmes it's often the case that only 3 or 4 are used regularly (the remainder ignored) and that I have found is often true of the microwave too. Check your handbook for detailed advice if you purchase such a model to get the best from it.

All that is required to install a portable microwave oven is a fused power socket. Manufacturers also recommend that you place the microwave on a stable surface and have adequate ventilation. It is therefore possible to site the microwave in a multitude of places. I place mine on a stable trolley so that I can wheel it from room to room as required – giving useful flexibility of cooking. Very handy at busy entertaining times like Christmas or even near an outside door when entertaining alfresco in the summer.

If you plan to build-in your microwave to kitchen units then ensure you buy the correct fixing kit or housing unit. Make sure there is adequate venting, and always check your microwave handbook for any special instructions.

Oven cleaning

Since the walls to the oven cavity of the microwave remain cool during cooking, cleaning is often a quick-wipe operation. Food does not have the opportunity to bake-on. Simply wipe, at regular intervals or as spills occur, with a damp soapy cloth – after disconnecting the oven from the electrical supply. Remove and wash oven trays, shelving and bases if possible in the same way, or according to the manufacturer's instructions.

Wipe over the outside surfaces and the door of the oven regularly but do not allow water to seep into the vents. If possible, also clean any air filters or stirrer fan guard according to the instructions in your handbook.

Stale cooking smells can be removed by boiling a solution of 3 parts water to 1 part lemon juice in a bowl in the microwave for about 5 minutes, then wipe with a cloth to dry.

Also remember to have the microwave checked or serviced by a qualified engineer every 12 months, or as recommended by the manufacturer.

Do not operate the cooker when it is empty. For safety, it's not a bad idea to place a cup of water in the cooker when it is not in use. If the cooker is accidentally switched on the water will absorb the energy – there is then negligible risk of damaging the magnetron.

Guide to comparative microwave oven control settings

SETTINGS USED IN THESE RECIPES	SETTINGS VARIATIONS ON POPULAR MICROWAVE OVENS	APPROXIMATE % POWER INPUT	APPROXIMATE POWER OUTPUT IN WATTS	COOKING TIMES (IN MINUTES) (FOR TIMES GREATER THAN 10 MINUTES SIMPLY ADD TOGETHER THE FIGURES IN THE APPROPRIATE COLUMNS)									
	1 keep warm — low 2	25%	150W	4	8	12	16	20	24	28	32	36	40
LOW	2 simmer 3	30%	200W	3¼	6¾	10	13¼	16¾	20	23¼	26¾	30	33¼
DEFROST	3 stew — medium/low 4	40%	250W	2½	5	7½	10	12½	15	17½	20	22½	25
	4 defrost — medium 5	50%	300W	2	4	6	8	10	12	14	16	18	20
MEDIUM	5 bake — medium 6	60%	400W	1¾	3¼	5	6¾	8¼	10	12	13 ¼	15	16½
	6 roast — high 7-8	75%	500-525W	1¼	2¾	4	5¼	6¾	8	9¼	10¾	12	13¼
HIGH	7 full/high — normal 10	100%	700W	1	2	3	4	5	6	7	8	9	10

Factors which affect microwave cooking

Starting temperature of food

Foods which are cooked from room temperature will take less time than foods which are frozen or chilled. Cooking times given in these recipes refer to a starting temperature of foods as they are normally stored, unless otherwise stated.

Density of food

The denser the food, the longer it takes to cook. Heavy, dense foods like meat or potatoes will take longer to cook than light, porous foods like sponge cakes and puddings. For the same reason a solid, dense mass of meat like a joint will take longer to cook than the same meat minced or chopped prior to cooking.

Composition of food

Foods which are high in fats and sugars will cook faster than foods high in liquid because fats and sugars absorb microwave energy more readily. They also reach higher temperatures during cooking than water-based foods. It therefore takes more time to cook foods which are high in moisture like meats and vegetables, than it does to cook those with little moisture like cakes and breads.

Quantity of food

As the volume or quantity of food being cooked in the microwave increases, the cooking time increases. Generally, if you double the amount of food the time will increase by about one half as much again, but do follow specific timings in recipes for success, and err on the side of safety – you can always add extra time but not take it away.

Size and shape of food

Smaller pieces of food will cook more quickly than larger pieces, and uniformly shaped pieces cook more evenly than irregularly shaped ones. With unevenly shaped pieces, the thinner parts will cook faster than the thicker areas and should be placed towards the centre of the dish where they receive less energy.

Ideally portions of food that are of the same size and shape cook most evenly. It is also important to remember that round and ring shapes cook more evenly than square, oval or rectangular shapes. With the latter the energy seems to concentrate in the corners and can cause charring – to overcome this affect, protect the corners with small pieces of foil to shield them from the energy (see 'shielding' on page 17).

Height in the oven

Areas that are closest to any source of energy cook faster than those further away and this also occurs in the microwave. Depending on its design your microwave may cook faster near the floor or roof. Rotating, turning over and stirring of foods will minimise this effect.

Bones in meat

Bone in meat conducts heat – therefore meat next to the bone in a joint or chop will cook first. Wherever possible, it is wise to bone and roll large pieces of meat for even cooking. If you don't, then remember to shield the meat next to the bone halfway through the cooking time to prevent over-cooking.

Techniques

As with any new appliance, and certainly with one that has an unfamiliar cooking action, there are a few simple techniques to follow to ensure success:

Stirring

Stirring is an operation that is carried out when cooking conventionally and is also applied when cooking by microwave. Conventionally we stir from the bottom of the pan to the top but with a microwave this is from the outside to the centre of a dish for even cooking. Precise stirring instructions will be given in a recipe if it is important, if not a simple stir halfway through cooking will suffice.

Rotating

If your model of microwave has a turntable (and most sold today do have one) then this cooking technique becomes redundant. If it hasn't then a simple quarter or half-turn of a dish at regular intervals during the cooking time will ensure even cooking when a dish cannot be stirred or turned over.

Turning over

Many large dense items of food like potatoes often appreciate turning over after about half of the microwave cooking time to ensure good results.

Arranging

The careful arranging of food in a dish for microwave cooking can mean the difference between a perfectly cooked ingredient and an adequately cooked one. For success follow the guidelines below:

- try to cook foods of an even or similar size together and if possible arrange in a ring pattern leaving the centre empty.
- if foods are of an irregular shape, like chops, spears of broccoli or small fish then arrange the thicker sections to the outside of the dish where they will receive the most energy to cook.
- for plated meals ensure the food is spread evenly across the plate or that thicker pieces of meat or vegetables are to the outer edge where they receive most energy.

◆ wherever possible ensure the depth of the food in a dish is even – if not, stir or rearrange to compensate for this.

Rearranging

Rearranging foods cooked in the microwave will also ensure evenly-cooked results – even if your microwave has a turntable. Once during the cooking time is usually sufficient – moving foods from the outside of the dish to the centre and vice versa.

Shielding

As with conventional cooking some parts of foods are more vulnerable to over-cooking than others. Wing tips of poultry, fish heads and tails, duck tail-ends and the narrow ends of legs of pork or lamb are examples. In such cases it is considered acceptable to introduce small strips of aluminium foil to protect such areas (although do check in your microwave handbook).

This is the ONLY TIME when metal may be introduced into a typical microwave oven and it is important to make sure it does not touch the oven walls. Position on the food for half of the cooking time and secure with wooden cocktail sticks if necessary.

Covering and wrapping

Drying out, spattering of walls and slower cooking times than needed can all be eliminated by covering or wrapping foods for the microwave. Covering will 'lock-in' and contain juices and speed up cooking times by trapping heat-retaining steam.

There are several ways to cover or wrap food for cooking:

◆ use a tight-fitting purpose made lid or an improvised saucer or plate for the same effect.

◆ use double-strength plastic cook bags especially for meat and vegetables but replace the metal ties with rubber bands, string or plastic clips.

◆ cover with a tight membrane of cling film but puncture or turn back a vent to prevent a 'ballooning' effect. Take care however when removing since it will trap steam which burns.

◆ use silicon lids that seal in the steam and protect against spatter. Make sure you lift them from the back to avoid scalding yourself with a gush of steam.

◆ use absorbent kitchen towel as a base to stand food on or as a cover for the same. It is especially good for absorbing excess moisture in foods that appreciate crisping like potatoes, bacon and bread. It is also invaluable for drying herbs and when dampened for reheating and steaming pancakes and shellfish.

Observing standing times

Food still continues to cook by conduction when microwave energy has been turned off. This is not a special action devoted to the microwave alone – the same action happens to a lesser degree with conventional cooking and it must be catered for. For this reason it is important to err on the side of safety and undercook rather than overcook food to allow for this action.

Removing excess cooking juices

Any juices that seep from a food will continue to attract microwave energy – if these juices are considerable then it is advisable to remove them with a bulb baster regularly during cooking so that they do not prolong cooking times appreciably.

Releasing pressure in foods

Foods with tight skins or membranes like sausages, kidneys, jacket potatoes, baked apples and egg yolks must be lightly pricked prior to cooking or they are liable to burst or explode. For the same reason boil-in-the-bag pouches and cling film must be cut or vented – this is because of the tremendous amount of pressure that develops within such quickly cooked food.

Browning foods

As a result of little applied surface heat over short cooking times – foods cooked in the microwave do not readily brown. To encourage and assist or disguise the browning process try one of the following tips if liked:

- grill foods like gratins and roasts before or after microwave cooking.
- use a special microwave browning dish especially for foods like chops, steaks, fried eggs, toasted sandwiches, stir-frys and chicken portions.
- buy or make your own browning mix to coat foods – paprika, toasted breadcrumbs, crushed crisps, soy sauce, Worcestershire sauce and soup mixes are good ideas that work well.
- bacon and pancetta due to their high fat content, brown readily so can be laid over poultry or roasts.

- baked items like cakes, biscuits and breads could be coated with toasted coconut, chocolate vermicelli, chopped nuts, chopped glacé fruits, poppy seeds, herbs and many dark coloured spices.
- ice or frost a cake or baked item after cooking.
- glaze ham, poultry or game with a fruit preserve or marmalade to add colour.

A few restrictions

The following foods do not cook well in the microwave:

Eggs in shells

These are liable to explode due to the build-up of pressure within the shell.

Batter recipes

Items like Yorkshire puddings, soufflés, pancakes and crêpes need conventional cooking to become crisp and firm.

Conventional meringues

These should be cooked in the conventional oven.

Deep fat frying

This is not recommended since it requires prolonged heating, it is difficult to control the temperature of the fat and food may burn.

Liquids in bottles

Check that bottles do not have too narrow necks or built-up pressure may cause them to shatter.

Dishes and utensils

Without doubt, the range of cooking utensils that can be used in the microwave oven is wider than those used for cooking conventionally.

A few exceptions do, however, exist. Most manufacturers object to the use of metal. Even small amounts in the oven will reflect the microwaves so that they do not penetrate the food to be cooked. Therefore, avoid metal dishes, baking trays and metal baking tins, foil dishes, cast-iron casseroles, plates and china trimmed with a metallic design, any dish with a metal screw or attachment and the paper-coated metal ties often found with freezer and cook bags.

Glass, pottery and china

Oven-proof and plain glass, pottery and china are all suitable. Be sure to check that they do not have any metallic trim, screws or handles, and if using a pottery dish, that it is non-porous. I have found that Pyrex dishes with in-built valves that you can open and shut in their 'Cook & Heat' range are excellent all-rounders. The steam valves work very well, and the cookware is suitable for the freezer, refrigerator, conventional oven and microwave so very multi-purpose. They are also dishwasher safe and stackable so save on storage space too.

Paper

For low heat and short cooking times, such as thawing, reheating or very short prime cooking, and for foods with a low fat, sugar or water content, paper is a good utensil. Napkins, paper towels, cups, cartons, paper freeze wrap and the paper pulp board often used for meat packaging are all suitable. (Paper towels are especially useful for cooking fatty foods, since they absorb excess fats and oils and can be used to prevent splattering on the walls of the oven.)

Wax-coated paper cups and plates should be avoided since the high temperature of the food will cause the wax to melt; they can, however, be used for defrosting cold items like frozen cakes and desserts.

Plastics

'Dishwasher Safe' is a useful indication as to whether or not a plastic is suitable for the microwave. Plastic dishes and containers, unless made of a thermoplastic material, should not be used for cooking food with a high fat or sugar content, since the heat of the food may cause the plastic to melt or lose its shape. Plastic film and devices like boil-in-bags work well.

Pierce the film or bag before cooking to allow steam to escape, and take care when removing the plastic film in case any steam remains. Do not attempt to cook in thin plastic bags as they will not withstand the heat of the food. Thicker storage bags are acceptable. Use elastic bands, string or non-metal ties to secure the bags loosely before cooking. Melamine is not recommended for microwave cooking since it absorbs enough microwave energy to cause charring.

Cotton and linen

Napkins are ideal for short warming or reheating procedures like reheating bread rolls for serving. It is important only to use cotton or linen containing no synthetic fibres.

Wooden bowls and basket ware

These are only suitable for short reheating purposes, otherwise the wood or wicker will tend to char, dry out or crack.

Roasting bags

A very clean, convenient way of cooking many foods. This is particularly true of meats, since browning takes place more readily within them than in other plastic bags. However, the metal ties must be replaced with elastic bands or string. Snip a couple of holes in the bag to aid the escape of steam.

Microwave containers

With the increased popularity of microwave cooking come a host of special innovations in microwave cookware. Several ranges manufactured from polythene, polystyrene and thermoplastics are now widely available and come in a comprehensive range of shapes and sizes.

Latest innovations mean that you can now purchase special microwave plate warmers, reheating domes, egg poachers, lidded microwave-safe saucepans, spatter guards, soup mugs, porridge bowls, hinged steam cases, quinoa and rice cookers, bacon crispers, omelette makers and a microwave grill to fit inside your microwave. If you wish to stack your food in the microwave there is also a multi-purpose tray that acts as a tray (to prevent scalded fingers), standing and cooling plate, plate stacker and splatter guard (it's also collapsible for easy storage).

Thermometers

Ones made especially for microwave ovens are available but can be used in an oven only when specified by that oven's manufacturer. To take the temperature reading with a standard meat thermometer, remove the food from the oven, insert the thermometer into the thickest portion of food and let it stand for about 10 minutes to register the internal temperature. If more cooking is needed, remove the thermometer and return the meat to the oven. Some newer ovens have an automatic cooking control, a temperature sensing probe that can be inserted into a roast or other food while in the oven. When the food reaches a precise temperature, the oven turns itself off automatically.

Browning dishes

Available from most microwave dealers, these duplicate the conventional browning and searing processes of conventional cooking. Especially useful for pre browning meat, poultry and fish, they can also be used for 'frying' eggs and sandwiches, and browning vegetables. The browning dish, made of a glass ceramic substance with a special coating that absorbs microwave energy, is preheated in the microwave until the base coating changes colour, usually about 8 minutes on HIGH or full power. The food is then placed on the dish to brown and turned to sear the remaining sides. Preheating times and browning or searing times differ according to the food being cooked and the power output of the oven. Always follow the manufacturer's instructions.

Remember

If you are going to cook food in both the microwave and the conventional oven, be sure to use an oven-proof dish. Here's a simple test:

Fill a heatproof glass cup with water and place in the utensil being checked. Place the utensil in the microwave oven and cook for 1¼ minutes. If the water is warm in the cup and the utensil is cool, go ahead and use the utensil. If the utensil is warm or even hot and the water is still cool, or barely lukewarm, do not use it for microwave cooking.

The shape of dish to use

After checking the material of the dish or utensil, consider its shape, too. Ideally, the more regular the shape the better it is suited to microwave cooking, e.g. round shaped is better than an oval. A straight-sided container is better than a curved one, as the microwaves can penetrate more evenly. A large shallow dish is better than a small deep one as the food offers a greater surface area to the microwaves.

Defrosting

During the early introductory years of the domestic microwave it was frequently referred to as 'the unfreezer' since one of the major advantages and bonuses of owning a microwave was its ability to defrost food quickly and efficiently.

Capitalising on this effect many microwave manufacturers (if not all) these days have introduced a special DEFROST control or button to ensure good defrosting microwave action. This control programmes the microwave to introduce just the right amount of energy to defrost food without cooking it – it does so by turning on and off the power at regular intervals.

It is possible to simulate this action by turning a microwave without such a control manually on and off at regular intervals with rest periods in between but is rarely as successful and can be time-consuming.

Defrosting tips

- Defrost food slowly – never try to hurry the process or there is a danger of cooking the food or drying it out unnecessarily.
- Frozen foods wrapped in freezer foil or foil containers should be stripped of their covering and placed in a suitable dish for the microwave.
- Separate sausage links, blocks of foods and stacked items like layered pancakes and burgers as they defrost.
- As with cooking, prick, slash or vent membranes like cling film before defrosting.
- Turn foods over, stir or rearrange to ensure even defrosting at least once.
- Remove excess drip or thaw juices with a bulb baster during defrosting.
- Remove giblets from poultry and game cavities when they have thawed.
- Remove metal lids and open cartons before defrosting.
- Crisp items like breads, cakes and biscuits will appreciate sitting on absorbent kitchen towel during defrosting.
- Break up blocks of meat and fish and rearrange during defrosting or remove when thawed.
- Take into account the residual heat action of the microwave by defrosting large roasts and poultry birds until just icy – after standing for some 10-15 minutes they will defrost to a chilled state.
- Shield any vulnerable areas of foods like fish tails, poultry wings and chop bones with foil during defrosting as in cooking.
- Shield any parts of foods that are defrosting unnecessarily faster than others with small strips of foil – position on the food with wooden cocktail sticks.
- If you intend to defrost and cook in one operation straight from the freezer then follow all the guidelines on stirring, turning, rotating and rearranging foods, not forgetting to allow a standing time too.

Reheating

Most foods will reheat in the microwave cooker without loss of quality, flavour, colour and some nutrients. For best results follow the guidelines below:

- Arrange foods on a plate for reheating so that the thicker, denser and meatier portions are to the outer edge.
- Cover foods when reheating with a layer of cling film if there is no lid to retain moisture.
- When reheating, observe the standing time action to make maximum use of the microwave energy and to prevent overcooking.
- When reheating potatoes in their jackets, breads, pastry items and other moist foods, place on a sheet of paper towel so that it may absorb the moisture.
- Stir foods regularly while reheating. If stirring is not possible, then rotate the food or dish or re-arrange it.

Meal and menu planning

As a general rule for microwave cooking, cook the main course first. Most meat, poultry and fish dishes, especially those cooked in sauces, do improve upon standing and roasts are often easier to carve. If wrapped in aluminium foil during their standing time, they will often require no further reheating.

Obviously, cook foods that require a long standing time first. Last-minute or quick-cooking dishes can be cooked during that standing time.

For ease of preparation and cooking, prepare starters and desserts well ahead and reheat if necessary just before serving. A pudding that needs little attention can often be cooked while you are eating the starter and main course.

Menu planning and serving food perfectly cooked is an art that comes with experience. Your microwave cooker will help you through this trial and error time if you err on the side of safety. Dishes that have become lukewarm will quickly reheat with perfect freshness rather than having a dried-out look.

Certainly until you have got the measure of your microwave do not attempt to reheat, thaw or even cook more than one dish in the oven at the same time – it is easy to overestimate the time required and forget the composition of the dish so that foods cook unevenly.

Adapting recipes and scaling down to serve 1 and 2

Many of your favourite family recipes can be converted for use in the microwave simply by adjusting, and often shortening, the recipe cooking time. The ideal way to start to convert a recipe is to study the recipe carefully and check whether there are any familiar techniques in its method such as roasting, steaming or poaching that you can easily convert. Check that all the ingredients included can be cooked in the microwave and refer to procedures and times from other standard microwave recipes to work out your cooking times.

The following checklist will help you with conversion, but use it only as a guideline – rely upon your own judgement for best results.

* In general terms, foods cooked in the microwave take about one-quarter to one-third of the time they take when cooking conventionally. But do, however, allow for standing times.
* Check the cooking process regularly. Stir and rearrange foods if they appear to be cooking unevenly.
* Use less liquid when cooking items like stews, casseroles and soups and in cooking vegetables.
* Foods tend to rise higher during microwave cooking so, in general, choose larger containers.
* Reduce flavourings like herbs and spices by about one-third since the flavours of these seem to be brought out more strongly by microwave cooking.
* Wherever possible, cut food into small, even-sized pieces so that they are small and uniform for quick cooking.

Many microwave recipes produced by manufacturers are geared to serving 4 or more – but don't despair and discard your handbook, for such recipes can be halved, quartered or reduced further.

As a general guideline:

* If you wish to make a recipe for 4 serve only 2 then halve the amount of each ingredient given and microwave for about two-thirds of the given cooking time.
* If you wish to make a recipe for 4 serve only 1 then quarter the amount of each ingredient given and microwave for about one-third of the given cooking time.

- Always err on the side of safety by undercooking rather than overcooking, especially with delicate egg, fish or cream dishes.
- Choose smaller cooking dishes but stir, turn, rotate or rearrange just as frequently.
- Leave to stand for 3-5 minutes after cooking to observe standing times rather than the 5-10 minutes usually recommended.

A few basics and some shortcuts

There are some staples and basics that you may want to cook frequently to use in recipes, serve as side dishes or use as accompaniments. Likewise there are some shortcuts that will come in handy for food preparation. Here are a few:

Bacon

To cook and crisp bacon (both back and streaky), place 4 rashers between sheets of absorbent kitchen paper and microwave on HIGH for 3½-4 minutes. The bacon will crisp up as it cools.

Butter

To soften, place 100 g/4 oz butter in a dish and microwave on HIGH for 15-30 seconds, watching constantly. To melt 25 g/1 oz microwave on HIGH for 30 seconds.

Caramel

To make caramel place 50 g/2 oz sugar in a large heatproof bowl with 2 tbsp water. Microwave on HIGH for 3½-4 minutes, stirring once after 1 minute and watching carefully after 3 minutes of the cooking time to prevent burning. Pour into an oiled dish (for crème caramel for example) or onto an oiled sheet for caramel pieces. Leave until cold and set.

Chocolate

To melt plain dessert chocolate, break 50 g/2 oz chocolate into pieces and place in a bowl. Microwave on MEDIUM for 2-2½ minutes, stirring twice until smooth.

Herbs and fruit slices

Lay herbs or fruit slices on a piece of absorbent kitchen paper and microwave on HIGH at 20 second bursts until all the moisture has evaporated. Allow to cool.

Honey

To soften or melt/revitalise crystallised or hardened honey, place 2 tbsp in a bowl and microwave on HIGH for 10 seconds. Alternatively microwave a 450 g/1 lb jar on HIGH for 1½-2 minutes, stirring once.

Ice cream

To soften hard (not soft-scoop) ice cream for serving, microwave in the container on MEDIUM for ½-1½ minutes (depending upon quantity). Leave to stand, covered for 1 minute before slicing or scooping to serve.

Lemons

To gain maximum yield when squeezing a lemon, prick the skin of the fruit then microwave on HIGH for 5-10 seconds before squeezing.

Nuts and seeds

To toast nuts and seeds, spread them out in a single layer on the turntable or a plate. Microwave on HIGH in 20 second bursts, stirring well each time, until they look and smell roasted.

Pasta

Pre-cooking dried lasagne for layering with meat or vegetable mixtures: Place 225 g/8 oz dried lasagne sheets in a large rectangular dish with 750 ml/1¼ pints boiling water and a pinch of salt. Cover and microwave on HIGH for 7-9 minutes, rearranging the sheets once. Drain and rinse under cold running water to use.

Fresh Pasta: Place 225 g/8 oz fresh pasta in a dish with a little oil and 750 ml/1¼ pints boiling water. Cover and microwave on HIGH for 2-3 minutes. Drain and use as required.

Dried Spaghetti: Break spaghetti in half and place in a dish with 1.2 litres/2 pints boiling water and a little oil.

Microwave, uncovered, on HIGH for 10-12 minutes, stirring once. Leave to stand for 2 minutes before draining to serve or use.

Potatoes

Mash: Place 150 g/5 oz peeled and diced potato (sufficient to serve 1) in a dish with 50 ml/2 fl oz water. Cover and microwave on HIGH for 4½-5 minutes. Drain well, add a generous knob of butter and mash to a smooth consistency. Add a little extra milk to loosen if required and season to taste to serve.

Jacket Potatoes: Scrub 175 g/6 oz potatoes and prick the skin. Place on a double sheet of absorbent kitchen paper. Microwave 1 x 175 g/6 oz potato on HIGH for 4-6 minutes and 2 x 175 g/6 oz potatoes on HIGH for 6-8 minutes, turning over once. Leave to stand for 3-4 minutes before serving.

Rice

Long-grain White Rice: Place 100 g/4 oz long-grain white rice in a cooking dish with 300 ml/½ pint boiling water, a little salt and knob of butter. Cover loosely and microwave on HIGH for 3 minutes. Reduce the power setting to MEDIUM and microwave for a further 12 minutes, stirring twice. Leave to stand, covered, for 5 minutes before serving. Fluff the rice with a fork to separate to serve.

Long-grain Brown Rice: Place 100 g/4 oz long-grain brown rice in a cooking dish with 300 ml/½ pint boiling water, a little salt and knob of butter. Cover loosely and microwave on HIGH for 3 minutes. Reduce the power setting to MEDIUM and microwave for a further 20 minutes, stirring twice. Leave to stand, covered, for 5 minutes before serving. Fluff the rice with a fork to separate to serve.

Guide to the recipes

All recipes have been tried, tested and developed for serving 1 or 2 people – however, some of the sauce recipes would prove too small and unworkable if reduced further. Any of these can be stored in the refrigerator for up to 24 hours then reheated for serving with other dishes.

All recipes in this book were created and tested using microwave ovens with a maximum power output of 700 watts. The ovens also had variable power and the descriptions used refer to the following power outputs:

HIGH = 700 watts or 100%

MEDIUM = 400 watts or 60%

DEFROST = 250 watts or 40%

LOW = 200 watts or 30%

The chart on page 14 gives the approximate power in watts at these levels and their relative cooking times.

The microwave ovens used for testing also had a turntable facility – if yours does not then follow the rules on turning, rotating and re-arranging in the introductory chapter.

Metric measurements may vary from one recipe to another within the book and it is essential to follow either metric or Imperial. The recipes have been carefully balanced to get the very best results using only one set of measures and cannot be interchanged.

Note that unless otherwise stated flour is of the plain variety, eggs used refer to size medium and all spoon quantities are measured level unless otherwise stated.

BREAKFASTS, STARTERS, LIGHT MEALS AND SNACKS

Plain and posh porridge

I think the recipe title gives the game away here – the basic recipe is for a plain oat porridge, but it can be made luxurious with the introduction of spices, different milks and fruit additions like grated citrus zest or dried fruit. But then you can go fully overboard with toppings of nuts, seeds, granola and any number of fruits and their combos when cooked so that breakfast never becomes 'samey'.

FOR ONE		FOR TWO
35 g/1½ oz	traditional porridge oats	75 g/3 oz
200 ml/7 fl oz	milk	400 ml/14 fl oz

For one ——

- Place the porridge oats and the milk in a measuring jug or large bowl (minimum capacity 600 ml/1 pint to allow for bubbling up and expansion during cooking). Add any flavourings if required at this stage. Microwave uncovered on HIGH for 2 minutes 40 seconds. This timing is based on using chilled semi-skimmed cow's milk – other milks and their temperatures may affect this timing – err on the side of safety and reduce then add extra time if you are unsure. The porridge mixture will bubble right to the top of the jug or bowl during cooking.
- Remove from the microwave and stir very well. Return and microwave uncovered on HIGH for a further 20-25 seconds until cooked and creamy.
- Stir well and pour into a serving bowl then top with any chosen topping accompaniments to serve.

For two ⎯⎯

- Place the porridge oats and the milk in a measuring jug or large bowl (minimum capacity of about 1 litre/2 pints to allow for bubbling up and expansion during cooking). Add any flavourings if required at this stage. Microwave uncovered on HIGH for 5 minutes. This timing is based on using chilled semi-skimmed cow's milk – other milks and their temperatures may affect this timing – err on the side of safety and reduce then add extra time if you are unsure. The porridge mixture will bubble right to the top of the jug or bowl during cooking.
- Remove from the microwave and stir very well. Return and microwave uncovered on HIGH for a further 30-40 seconds until cooked and creamy.
- Stir well and pour into 2 serving bowls then top with any chosen topping accompaniments to serve.

Pizza style breakfast muffins

Pizza for breakfast? Why not! But this one is in the guise of a muffin. Chorizo (or pepperoni), cheese, tomatoes, anchovies, herbs and black olives nestle here in a light egg muffin mixture that is cooked in a tulip wrap muffin case set inside a large breakfast mug. It's delicious warm but also good cold with a little salad if serving for brunch.

FOR ONE		FOR TWO
1	small egg(s)	2
30 ml/2 tbsp	milk	60 ml/4 tbsp
15 ml/1 tbsp	olive oil	30 ml/2 tbsp
60 ml/4 tbsp	plain flour	120 ml/8 tbsp
5 ml/1 tsp	baking powder	10 ml/2 tsp
10 ml/2 tsp	grated Parmesan cheese	20 ml/4 tsp
2.5 ml/½ tsp	dried oregano	5 ml/1 tsp
15 g/½ oz	chopped chorizo or pepperoni	25 g/1 oz
1	baby plum tomato(es), quartered	2
1	black olive(s), sliced	2
1	anchovy fillet(s), chopped	2
	salt and freshly ground black pepper	
15 ml/1 tbsp	grated Cheddar cheese	30 ml/2 tbsp

For one —

- Place the egg with the milk, oil, flour, baking powder, Parmesan cheese and oregano in a bowl or jug and beat with a fork to combine. Stir in the chorizo, tomato, black olives, anchovy and salt and pepper to taste, mixing well.
- Spoon into a tulip wrap muffin case set inside a large mug or cup (about 300 ml/½ pint capacity) and sprinkle with the Cheddar cheese.
- Microwave uncovered on HIGH for 1½ minutes, until well risen and cooked. Leave to stand for 1 minute before serving.

For two —

- Place the eggs with the milk, oil, flour, baking powder, Parmesan cheese and oregano in a bowl or jug and beat with a fork to combine. Stir in the chorizo, tomato, black olives, anchovies and salt and pepper to taste, mixing well.
- Spoon into two tulip wrap muffin cases set inside two large mugs or cups (about 300 ml/½ pint each in capacity) and sprinkle with the Cheddar cheese.
- Microwave uncovered on HIGH for 2½-3 minutes, until well risen and cooked. Leave to stand for 1 minute before serving.

Speedy Mexican huevos rancheros

This fabulous Mexican breakfast dish of eggs in a sauce of onion, peppers, tomato and spices really hits the spot early in the day. It is made using chipotle paste which can be a little bit fiery so add judiciously unless you really enjoy the heat of chillies. I like to serve with some bread – sourdough is my choice but tortillas might be more authentic.

FOR ONE		FOR TWO
30 ml/ 2 tbsp	olive oil	60 ml/4 tbsp
50 g/2 oz	yellow pepper, chopped	100 g/4 oz
25 g/1 oz	onion, chopped	50 g/2 oz
1	garlic clove(s), peeled and chopped	2
125 ml/4 fl oz	canned chopped tomatoes	250 ml/8 fl oz
15 ml/1 tbsp	dried oregano	30 ml/2 tbsp
5 ml/1 tsp	chipotle paste	10 ml/2 tsp
25 g/1 oz	fresh spinach, coarsely chopped	50 g/2 oz
30 ml/2 tbsp	fresh coriander leaves, chopped	60 ml/4 tbsp
1	egg(s)	2
	red chilli slices (optional)	

For one ⸻

- Place half of the olive oil, the yellow pepper, onion, garlic, chopped tomatoes, oregano and chipotle paste in bowl or cup, suitable for serving in. A large breakfast style cup or bowl works well. Cover and microwave on HIGH for 6 minutes, stirring halfway through the cooking time. The mixture will bubble and become very hot during this time so take extra care when removing any cover to stir.
- Add the spinach and half of the coriander, mixing well. Gently flatten the mixture with the back of a spoon then make a shallow hollow in the centre and crack in the egg. Drizzle with the remaining oil then re-cover.
- Microwave on HIGH for 1½-2 minutes depending upon the size of the egg being used and how you like your eggs cooked (the shorter time for a small egg and a runnier yolk). Leave to stand for 1 minute then sprinkle with the remaining coriander and a few slices of red chilli to serve.

For two ⸻

- Mix half of the olive oil, the yellow pepper, onion, garlic, chopped tomatoes, oregano and chipotle paste in bowl, then divide between 2 large mugs or bowls suitable for cooking and serving in. Two large breakfast style cup or bowls work well. Cover both and microwave on HIGH for 10 minutes, stirring halfway through the cooking time. The mixture will bubble and become very hot during this time so take extra care when removing any cover to stir.
- Divide the spinach and half of the coriander between each, mixing well. Gently flatten the mixture with the back of a spoon then make a shallow hollow in the centre of each and crack in the eggs. Drizzle with the remaining oil then re-cover.
- Microwave on HIGH for 2½-3¼ minutes depending upon the size of the eggs being used and how you like your eggs cooked (the shorter time for small eggs and a runnier yolk). Leave to stand for 1 minute then sprinkle with the remaining coriander and a few slices of red chilli to serve.

Magical shakshuka

This is just the sort of instant type breakfast or brunch dish that I turn to when cereal just doesn't appeal and plain eggs don't quite cut it. It's an egg perfectly cooked in a sauce of tomatoes, garlic and peppers topped with a little chopped coriander and simply perfect with some sourdough toast for dipping. The red pepper salsa is something of a must (and choose a good quality one) but can be replaced with ¼-½ chopped red pepper.

FOR ONE		FOR TWO
5 ml/1 tsp	olive oil	10 ml/2 tsp
200 ml/7 fl oz	tomato passata	400 ml/14 fl oz
½	garlic clove, crushed	1
20 ml/4 tsp	red pepper salsa	40 ml/8 tsp
	salt and freshly ground black pepper	
1	egg(s)	2
15 ml/1 tbsp	chopped fresh coriander leaves	30 ml/2 tbsp

For one ——

- ◆ Brush a large breakfast style cup or bowl with half of the oil.
- ◆ Mix the passata with the garlic, salsa and salt and pepper to taste and add to the bowl or cup. Make a small hollow or gently flatten the mixture with the back of a spoon in the centre and crack in the egg. Drizzle with the remaining oil and cover.
- ◆ Microwave on HIGH for 1 minute then in 20 second bursts until the white is just set and the egg is cooked to your liking. Leave to stand for 1 minute, then sprinkle with the coriander to serve.

For two ——

- ◆ Brush 2 large breakfast style cups or bowls with half of the oil.
- ◆ Mix the passata with the garlic, salsa and salt and pepper to taste and divide between the cups or bowls. Make a small hollow or gently flatten the mixture with the back of a spoon in the centre and crack an egg into each. Drizzle with the remaining oil and cover.
- ◆ Microwave on HIGH for 1¾ minutes then in 20 second bursts until the whites are just set and the eggs are cooked to your liking. Leave to stand for 1 minute, then sprinkle with the coriander to serve.

Country pâté

A simple chicken liver pâté made all the more special by using ready-blended herbs and garlic butter.

FOR ONE		FOR TWO
50 g/2 oz	chicken livers, trimmed	100 g/4 oz
½	small onion, peeled and chopped	1
25 g/1 oz	savoury herbs and garlic butter	50 g/2 oz

For one ——

* Place the chicken livers, onion and half of the butter in a bowl. Cover and microwave on HIGH for 1-1½ minutes until cooked. Mash with a fork until as smooth as possible. Spoon into a small ramekin or dish.
* Place the remaining butter in a dish and microwave on HIGH for ¼ minute to melt. Spoon over the pâté and chill until set.
* Serve cold with warm toast fingers and a salad garnish.

For two ——

* Place the chicken livers, onion and half of the butter in a bowl. Cover and microwave on HIGH for 1½-2 minutes until cooked. Mash with a fork until as smooth as possible. Spoon into a small ramekin or dish.
* Place the remaining butter in a dish and microwave on HIGH for ¼ minute to melt. Spoon over the pâté and chill until set.
* Serve cold with warm toast fingers and a salad garnish.

Leanline chicken and orange pâté

Calorie counters and weight watchers will be pleased to note that this tasty pâté costs only 140 calories from a daily allowance. Serve with raw vegetable sticks or toasted low-calorie bread.

FOR ONE		FOR TWO
7 g/¼ oz	low-fat spread	15 g/½ oz
½	small onion, peeled and chopped	1
50 g/2 oz	cooked chicken, skin removed and chopped	100 g/4 oz
7.5 ml/1½ tsp	unsweetened orange juice	15 ml/1 tbsp
5 ml/1 tsp	finely chopped fresh parsley	10 ml/2 tsp
45 ml/3 tbsp	natural yogurt	75 ml/5 tbsp
25 g/1 oz	button mushrooms, wiped and sliced	50 g/2 oz
¼	small green pepper, cored, seeded and finely chopped	½
	salt and freshly ground black pepper	

For one ——

* Place the low-fat spread and onion in a bowl. Cover and microwave on HIGH for ¾-1 minute.
* Place the onion mixture, chicken and orange juice in a blender and process on a low speed until finely chopped.
* Add the parsley and yogurt and blend again to mix.
* Remove from the blender and fold in the mushrooms, green pepper and salt and pepper to taste.
* Spoon into a small dish and chill thoroughly before serving with raw vegetable sticks or toast.

For two ——

* Place the low-fat spread and onion in a bowl. Cover and microwave on HIGH for 1-1½ minutes.
* Place the onion mixture, chicken and orange juice in a blender and process on a low speed until finely chopped.
* Add the parsley and yogurt and blend again to mix.

- Remove from the blender and fold in the mushrooms, green pepper and salt and pepper to taste.
- Spoon into a small dish and chill thoroughly before serving with raw vegetable sticks or toast.

Save and savour

Leanline Chicken and Orange Pâté is a tasty way to use up cooked leftover chicken or turkey.

Quick kipper pâté

A lemony kipper pâté that is best served chilled with warm Melba toast or crackers.

FOR ONE		FOR TWO
50 g/2 oz	boneless kipper fillets	100 g/4 oz
15 g/½ oz	softened butter	25 g/1 oz
2.5 ml/½ tsp	finely grated lemon rind	5 ml/1 tsp
	pinch of ground nutmeg	
	salt and freshly ground black pepper	

For one ——

- Place the kipper fillets in a small bowl and microwave on HIGH for 1-1½ minutes or until cooked.
- Remove any skin and discard. Add the butter, lemon rind, nutmeg and salt and pepper to taste. Mash well with a fork until well blended.
- Spoon into a small ramekin or dish and chill until set.
- Serve lightly chilled with Melba toast or crackers.

For two ——

- Place the kipper fillets in a small bowl and microwave on HIGH for 2-2½ minutes or until cooked.
- Remove any skin and discard. Add the butter, lemon rind, nutmeg and salt and pepper to taste. Mash well with a fork until well blended.
- Spoon into a small ramekin or dish and chill until set.
- Serve lightly chilled with Melba toast or crackers.

Prawns in spicy garlic butter

Large unshelled Mediterranean prawns are best for this but if unavailable use peeled prawns instead.

FOR ONE		FOR TWO
7.5 ml/1½ tsp	olive oil	15 ml/1 tbsp
7 g/¼ oz	butter	15 g/½ oz
1	garlic clove(s), peeled and thinly sliced	2
1.25 ml/¼ tsp	ground paprika	2.5 ml/½ tsp
1.25 ml/¼ tsp	ground cumin	2.5 ml/½ tsp
	pinch of ground ginger	
100 g/4 oz	large unshelled Mediterranean prawns	225 g/8 oz
7.5 ml/1½ tsp	chopped fresh parsley	15 ml/1 tbsp
7.5 ml/1½ tsp	snipped chives	15 ml/1 tbsp

For one —

* Place the oil, butter and garlic in a shallow cooking dish and microwave on HIGH for ½-¾ minute until the butter is melted.
* Stir in the paprika, cumin and ginger, blending well.
* Add the prawns and toss well to coat in the spicy garlic butter.
* Microwave on HIGH for 2 minutes, stirring twice.
* Stir in the parsley and chives and serve at once, with French bread.

For two —

* Place the oil, butter and garlic in a shallow cooking dish and microwave on HIGH for 1-1¼ minutes until the butter is melted.
* Stir in the paprika, cumin and ginger, blending well.
* Add the prawns and toss well to coat in the spicy garlic butter.
* Microwave on HIGH for 3-4 minutes, stirring twice.
* Stir in the parsley and chives and serve at once, with French bread.

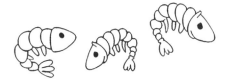

Mushrooms à la Grecque

A light mushroom starter with wine and tomatoes. Serve cold with warm crusty bread.

FOR ONE		FOR TWO
½	small onion, peeled and finely chopped	1
½	medium carrot, peeled and finely chopped	1
5 ml/1 tsp	olive oil	10 ml/ 2 tsp
30 ml/2 tbsp	dry white wine	60 ml/4 tbsp
1	bouquet garni	1
50 g/2 oz	button mushrooms, wiped	100 g/4 oz
2	tomatoes, skinned, seeded and chopped	4
	salt and freshly ground black pepper	
	chopped fresh parsley, to garnish	

For one

* Place the onion, carrot and oil in a bowl. Cover and microwave on HIGH for 1-1½ minutes.
* Add the wine and bouquet garni. Cover, reduce the power setting and microwave on MEDIUM for 2 minutes.
* Add the mushrooms, tomatoes and salt and pepper to taste, blending well. Microwave, uncovered, on MEDIUM for 5 minutes, stirring once.
* Remove and discard the bouquet garni and leave to cool. Garnish with parsley and serve chilled.

For two

* Place the onion, carrot and oil in a bowl. Cover and microwave on HIGH for 2-3 minutes.
* Add the wine and bouquet garni. Cover, reduce the power setting and microwave on MEDIUM for 3½ minutes.
* Add the mushrooms, tomatoes and salt and pepper to taste, blending well. Microwave, uncovered, on MEDIUM for 8-9 minutes, stirring once.
* Remove and discard the bouquet garni and leave to cool. Garnish with parsley and serve chilled.

Sardine, avocado and corn starter

A good economical alternative to a prawn cocktail to start a meal. More of a pâté than a fish cocktail. Serve with fingers of warm wholemeal toast.

FOR ONE		FOR TWO
15 g/½ oz	butter	25 g/1 oz
¼	small onion, peeled and finely chopped	½
1.25 ml/¼ tsp	French mustard	2.5 ml/½ tsp
½ x 125 g/4½ oz	can sardines in oil, drained and bones removed	1 x 125 g/4½ oz
15 ml/1 tbsp	cream cheese	30 ml/2 tbsp
¼	avocado, peeled, stoned and mashed	½
	dash of lemon juice	
	salt and freshly ground black pepper	
75 g/3 oz	canned sweetcorn kernels	175 g/6 oz
	shredded lettuce	
	parsley sprigs, to garnish	

For one

* Place the butter and onion in a bowl. Microwave on HIGH for 1 minute. Leave until cold and almost set.
* Mix the onion butter with the mustard, sardines, cream cheese and avocado, blending well.
* Add lemon juice and salt and pepper to taste and fold in half of the sweetcorn.
* Pile onto a bed of shredded lettuce and sprinkle with the remaining sweetcorn. Garnish with sprigs of parsley and serve at once with wholemeal bread.

For two

* Place the butter and onion in a bowl. Microwave on HIGH for 1½ minutes. Leave until cold and almost set.
* Mix the onion butter with the mustard, sardines, cream cheese and avocado, blending well.
* Add lemon juice and salt and pepper to taste and fold in half of the sweetcorn.
* Pile onto a bed of shredded lettuce and sprinkle with the remaining sweetcorn. Garnish with sprigs of parsley and serve at once with wholemeal bread.

Isle of Skye soup

Bit of a cheat really but no-one would know that this expensive-tasting mushroom and whisky soup is based on an economical can.

FOR ONE		FOR TWO
1 x 435 g (15 oz)	small cans creamed mushroom soup	2 x 435 g (15 oz)
15 ml/1 tbsp	whisky (Talisker if possible)	30 ml/2 tbsp
15 ml/1 tbsp	single cream	30 ml/2 tbsp
1	button mushroom(s), sliced to garnish (optional)	2

For one

* Place the soup in a bowl. Microwave on HIGH for 2-3 minutes, stirring once.
* Place the whisky in a soup bowl and pour over the soup.
* Swirl the cream on top of the soup and garnish with the sliced mushroom. Serve at once.

For two

* Place the soup in a bowl. Microwave on HIGH for 3-4 minutes, stirring once.
* Place the whisky in 2 soup bowls and pour over the soup.
* Swirl the cream on top of the soup and garnish with the sliced mushroom. Serve at once.

Crab and sweetcorn soup

I first sampled this Chinese style soup as a student when assisting the great authority on Chinese cuisine, Kenneth Lo. I have changed and adapted it many times over the years – here is the tasty microwave version.

FOR ONE		FOR TWO
150 ml/¼ pint	chicken stock	300 ml/½ pint
50 g/2 oz	canned sweetcorn kernels	100 g/4 oz
25 g/1 oz	cooked chicken, cut into thin strips	50 g/2 oz
25 g/1 oz	canned or fresh crabmeat, flaked	50 g/2 oz
1.25 ml/¼ tsp	grated fresh root ginger	2.5 ml/½ tsp
5 ml/1 tsp	cornflour	10 ml/2 tsp
	salt and freshly ground black pepper	
5 ml/1 tsp	dry sherry	10 ml/2 tsp
	chopped spring onions, to garnish	

For one ——

- Place the chicken stock, sweetcorn, chicken, crab and ginger in a bowl. Cover and microwave on HIGH for 1½ minutes.
- Mix the cornflour to a smooth paste with a little water. Stir into the soup with salt and pepper to taste, blending well.
- Microwave on HIGH for ½-1 minute, stirring twice until clear and thickened.
- Stir in the sherry and sprinkle with chopped spring onions to garnish. Serve hot.

For two ——

- Place the chicken stock, sweetcorn, chicken, crab and ginger in a bowl. Cover and microwave on HIGH for 3 minutes.
- Mix the cornflour to a smooth paste with a little water. Stir into the soup with salt and pepper to taste, blending well.
- Microwave on HIGH for 1-1½ minutes, stirring twice until clear and thickened.
- Stir in the sherry and sprinkle with chopped spring onions to garnish. Serve hot.

Fresh tomato and herb soup

Without doubt this full-flavoured tomato soup will spoil you to never want a canned variety again - vary the herbs.

FOR ONE		FOR TWO
7 g/¼ oz	butter	15 g/½ oz
½	small onion, peeled and chopped	1
3.5 ml/¾ tsp	flour	7.5 ml/1½ tsp
175 g/6 oz	tomatoes, skinned, seeded and chopped	350 g/12 oz
2.5 ml/½ tsp	chopped fresh mixed herbs	5 ml/1 tsp
175 ml/6 fl oz	chicken stock	350 ml/ 12 fl oz
5 ml/1 tsp	tomato purée	10 ml/2 tsp
1	bay leaf	1
	salt and freshly ground black pepper	
10 ml/2 tsp	milk	15 ml/1 tbsp
	fresh herbs, to garnish	

For one

- Place the butter and onion in a bowl. Cover and microwave on HIGH for 1½ minutes, stirring once.
- Add the flour, blending well then gradually add the tomatoes, herbs, stock, tomato purée and bay leaf, blending well.
- Cook, uncovered, on HIGH for 2 minutes, stirring once. Add salt and pepper to taste, blending well. Microwave on HIGH for a further 1-1½ minutes.
- Remove and discard the bay leaf. Purée the soup in a blender or push through a fine sieve.
- Stir in the milk and microwave on HIGH for 1½-2 minutes until hot, stirring twice. Serve hot.

For two

- Place the butter and onion in a bowl. Cover and microwave on HIGH for 2 minutes, stirring once.
- Add the flour, blending well then gradually add the tomatoes, herbs, stock, tomato purée and bay leaf, blending well.
- Cook, uncovered, on HIGH for 4 minutes, stirring once. Add salt and pepper to taste, blending well. Microwave on HIGH for a further 2-3 minutes.
- Remove and discard the bay leaf. Purée the soup in a blender or push through a fine sieve.
- Stir in the milk and microwave on HIGH for 3-4 minutes until hot, stirring twice. Serve hot.

Creamed mushroom and bacon soup

This soup is delicious served with hot butter-flavoured bread – herb or lemon are a good choice.

FOR ONE		FOR TWO
15 g/½ oz	butter	25 g/1 oz
50 g/2 oz	mushrooms, wiped and sliced	100 g/4 oz
¼	small onion, peeled and chopped	½
15 g/½ oz	flour	25 g/1 oz
100 ml/ 4 fl oz	milk	200 ml/7 fl oz
75 ml/5 tbsp	chicken stock	150 ml/¼ pint
	salt and freshly ground black pepper	
25 g/ 1 oz	bacon, rinded	50 g/2 oz

For one —

* Place the butter in a bowl and microwave on HIGH for ½ minute to melt. Add the mushrooms and onion, blending well. Cover and cook on HIGH for 1½-2 minutes.
* Blend the flour with a little of the milk to make a smooth paste. Gradually stir in the remaining milk and stock. Add to the mushroom mixture with salt and pepper to taste, blending well.
* Microwave on HIGH for 2 minutes, stirring twice.
* Purée in a blender or push through a fine sieve.
* Meanwhile place the bacon on a plate and cover with absorbent kitchen towel. Microwave on HIGH for 1-2 minutes until crisp. Allow to cool slightly then crumble coarsely.
* Reheat the soup on HIGH for 1 minute. Serve hot sprinkled with crumbled bacon.

For two —

* Place the butter in a bowl and microwave on HIGH for ½ minute to melt. Add the mushrooms and onion, blending well. Cover and cook on HIGH for 1½-2 minutes.
* Blend the flour with a little of the milk to make a smooth paste. Gradually stir in the remaining milk and stock. Add to the mushroom mixture with salt and pepper to taste, blending well.
* Microwave on HIGH for 2 minutes, stirring twice.
* Purée in a blender or push through a fine sieve.
* Meanwhile place the bacon on a plate and cover with absorbent kitchen towel. Microwave on HIGH for 1-2 minutes until crisp. Allow to cool slightly then crumble coarsely.
* Reheat the soup on HIGH for 1 minute. Serve hot sprinkled with crumbled bacon.

Brandied French onion soup

It is essential to use a good home-made beef stock in this soup recipe – when in a hurry use canned beef consommé.

FOR ONE		FOR TWO
15 g/½ oz	butter	25 g/1 oz
1	medium onion(s), peeled and thinly sliced	2
	pinch of caster sugar	
2.5 ml/½ tsp	flour	5 ml/1 tsp
250 ml/9 fl oz	rich beef stock	450 ml/¾ pint
	salt and freshly ground black pepper	
1	slice(s) toasted French bread	2
25 g/1 oz	grated cheese	50 g/2 oz
10 ml/2 tsp	brandy	15 ml/1 tbsp

For one —

- Place the butter in a bowl and microwave on HIGH for ½ minute to melt. Add the onions and microwave, uncovered, on HIGH for 2-2½ minutes, stirring once.
- Add the sugar, blending well and microwave on HIGH for 1 minute.
- Add the flour then gradually stir in the stock or beef consommé and salt and pepper to taste. Microwave, uncovered, for 3½ minutes.
- Meanwhile sprinkle the toast with the cheese.
- Stir the brandy into the soup, blending well. Pour the soup into a soup bowl, float the cheese slice on top and microwave on HIGH for 1-2 minutes until the soup is hot and the cheese has melted.

For two —

- Place the butter in a bowl and microwave on HIGH for ¾ minute to melt. Add the onions and microwave, uncovered, on HIGH for 3-4 minutes, stirring once.
- Add the sugar, blending well and microwave on HIGH for 1½ minutes.
- Add the flour then gradually stir in the stock or beef consommé and salt and pepper to taste. Microwave, uncovered, for 7 minutes.
- Meanwhile sprinkle the toast with the cheese.
- Stir the brandy into the soup, blending well. Pour the soup into a soup bowl, float the cheese slice on top and microwave on HIGH for 2-3 minutes until the soup is hot and the cheese has melted.

Storecupboard standby

This can be easily made in the spur of the moment from a well-stocked storecupboard in half the time it would take to make conventionally.

Minestrone with Parmesan

A nourishing and colourful Italian soup.

FOR ONE		FOR TWO
15 g/½ oz	butter	25 g/1 oz
40 g/1½ oz	chopped carrots	75 g/3 oz
40 g/1½ oz	chopped celery	75 g/3 oz
40 g/1½ oz	diced potato	75 g/3 oz
½	small onion, peeled and sliced	1
½ x 225 g/8 oz	can tomatoes, drained and chopped	1 x 225 g/8 oz
15 g/½ oz	short cut macaroni	25 g/1 oz
7 g/¼ oz	flour	15 g/½ oz
250 ml/9 fl oz	beef stock	450 ml/¾ pint
	salt and freshly ground black pepper	
15 ml/1 tbsp	frozen peas	30 ml/2 tbsp
	freshly grated Parmesan cheese, to serve	

For one ——

- ◆ Place the butter, carrots, celery, potato, onion, tomatoes and macaroni in a bowl. Cover and microwave on HIGH for 3½ minutes.
- ◆ Stir in the flour, blending well. Gradually add the stock and microwave, uncovered, for 3½ minutes.
- ◆ Season to taste with salt and pepper and add the peas. Microwave on HIGH for 1 minute. Cover and leave to stand for 5 minutes. Serve with Parmesan.

For two ——

- ◆ Place the butter, carrots, celery, potato, onion, tomatoes and macaroni in a bowl. Cover and microwave on HIGH for 7 minutes.
- ◆ Stir in the flour, blending well. Gradually add the stock and microwave, uncovered, for 7 minutes.
- ◆ Season to taste with salt and pepper and add the peas. Microwave on HIGH for 1½ minutes. Cover and leave to stand for 5 minutes. Serve with Parmesan.

Scrambled smoked salmon and eggs

There is no need to buy prime smoked salmon for this dish – look out for smoked salmon trimmings at your fish counter at a fraction of the price. You could also ring the changes by using thin sliced smoked tuna instead.

FOR ONE		FOR TWO
2	eggs, beaten	4
7.5 ml/1½ tsp	single cream	15 ml/1 tbsp
	salt and freshly ground black pepper	
50 g/2 oz	smoked salmon, chopped	100 g/4 oz
7.5 ml/1½ tsp	snipped fresh parsley or chives	15 ml/1 tbsp

For one ——

* Mix the eggs with the cream and salt and pepper to taste in a bowl. Microwave on HIGH for 1¾-2 minutes, stirring every ½ minute until just set and creamy.
* Stir in the smoked salmon pieces and parsley or chives, blending well.
* Serve at once with brown bread triangles.

For two ——

* Mix the eggs with the cream and salt and pepper to taste in a bowl. Microwave on HIGH for 3 minutes, stirring every ½ minute until just set and creamy.
* Stir in the smoked salmon pieces and parsley or chives, blending well.
* Serve at once with brown bread triangles.

Savoury baked eggs

Eggs baked with cream and pâté make a delicious starter to serve with hot toast fingers. Cook on DEFROST power to ensure that the egg is just lightly set.

FOR ONE		FOR TWO
25 g/1 oz	smooth spreading pâté	50 g/2 oz
1	large egg(s)	2
30 ml/2 tbsp	double cream	60 ml/4 tbsp
	salt and freshly ground black pepper	
	parsley sprigs, to garnish	

For one

- Spread the pâté over the base of a lightly greased ramekin dish.
- Crack the egg over the pâté and carefully puncture the yolk with the tip of a knife.
- Spoon over the cream and season to taste with salt and pepper.
- Cover loosely with cling film and microwave on DEFROST for 3-3½ minutes until the egg is just set.
- Garnish with parsley sprigs and serve at once with hot toast fingers.

For two

- Spread the pâté over the base of two lightly greased ramekin dishes.
- Crack the eggs over the pâté and carefully puncture the yolks with the tip of a knife.
- Spoon over the cream and season to taste with salt and pepper.
- Cover loosely with cling film and microwave on DEFROST for 5-7 minutes until the eggs are just set.
- Garnish with parsley sprigs and serve at once with hot toast fingers.

Asparagus eggs

Asparagus makes an elegant entrance into this delightfully creamy egg starter. Use green rather than white asparagus for colour.

FOR ONE		FOR TWO
2	eggs, beaten	4
7.5 ml/1½ tsp	milk	15 ml/1 tbsp
	salt and freshly ground black pepper	
15 g/½ oz	butter	25 g/1 oz
3	cooked asparagus tips, chopped	6
7.5 ml/1½ tsp	snipped fresh chives	15 ml/1 tbsp

For one

- Mix the eggs with the milk and salt and pepper to taste in a bowl. Microwave on HIGH for 1¾-2 minutes, stirring every ½ minute until just set and creamy.
- Stir in the asparagus and chives, blending well.
- Serve at once with wholemeal toast fingers, if liked.

For two

- Mix the eggs with the milk and salt and pepper to taste in a bowl. Microwave on HIGH for 3 minutes, stirring every ½ minute until just set and creamy.
- Stir in the asparagus and chives, blending well.
- Serve at once with wholemeal toast fingers, if liked.

Moules marinière

Delicious and elegant, mussels make succulent eating when cooked the microwave way. Tightly covered and steamed in a little wine they retain their unique delicate flavour and texture.

FOR ONE		FOR TWO
300 ml/½ pint	mussels	600 ml/1 pint
15 g/½ oz	butter	25 g/1 oz
½	small onion, peeled and finely chopped	1
½	garlic clove, peeled and crushed	1
75 ml/5 tbsp	dry white wine	150 ml/¼ pint
	freshly ground black pepper	
	chopped fresh parsley, to garnish	

For one

- Wash and scrub the mussels removing the beards. Discard any mussels that are open.
- Place the butter, onion and garlic in a bowl and microwave on HIGH for 1½ minutes, stirring once.
- Add the wine and pepper to taste, blending well. Microwave on HIGH until the mixture boils, about 1½ minutes.
- Add the mussels, cover and microwave on HIGH for 1½-2 minutes or until the shells open. Discard any mussels whose shells do not open.
- Transfer to a serving dish, garnish with parsley and serve immediately.

For two

- Wash and scrub the mussels removing the beards. Discard any mussels that are open.
- Place the butter, onion and garlic in a bowl and microwave on HIGH for 2½ minutes, stirring once.

- Add the wine and pepper to taste, blending well. Microwave on HIGH until the mixture boils, about 2½ minutes.
- Add the mussels, cover and microwave on HIGH for 3-3½ minutes or until the shells open. Discard any mussels whose shells do not open.
- Transfer to a serving dish, garnish with parsley and serve immediately.

Pasta with cream and Parmesan

A classic pasta starter that is quick and easy to make. Double the portions and add chopped ham or tuna fish for a main course.

FOR ONE		FOR TWO
50 g/2 oz	dried pasta quills	100 g /4 oz
300 ml/½ pint	boiling chicken stock or water	450 ml/¾ pint
7 g/¼ oz	butter	15 g/½ oz
75 ml/5 tbsp	double cream	150 ml/¼ pint
	salt and freshly ground black pepper	
10 ml/2 tsp	grated Parmesan cheese	20 ml/4 tsp
	pinch of sweet paprika	

For one —

- Place the pasta in a deep bowl with the boiling stock. Cover and microwave on HIGH for 12-14 minutes then allow to stand for 5-10 minutes.
- While the pasta is standing, place the butter, cream and salt and pepper to taste in a bowl. Microwave on HIGH for 1 minute until hot, stirring once.
- Drain the cooked pasta and place on a serving plate. Spoon over the cream sauce and toss gently together to mix.
- Sprinkle with the Parmesan cheese and paprika and serve at once.

For two —

- Place the pasta in a deep bowl with the boiling stock. Cover and microwave on HIGH for 12-14 minutes then allow to stand for 5-10 minutes.
- While the pasta is standing, place the butter, cream and salt and pepper to taste in a bowl. Microwave on HIGH for 1-1½ minutes until hot, stirring once.
- Drain the cooked pasta and place on a serving plate. Spoon over the cream sauce and toss gently together to mix.
- Sprinkle with the Parmesan cheese and paprika and serve at once.

Storecupboard standby

Pasta with cream and Parmesan can easily be made on the spur of the moment from a well-stocked storecupboard and refrigerator.

Seconds out for Spaghetti Carbonara

Who doesn't like Spaghetti Carbonara? Who hasn't been disappointed with shop-bought meals for one or two on this pasta variation? No-one, which is why I have attempted (and I think succeeded) in making an authentic microwave version to cook at home. It's here but it should be noted that the timings and the order of cooking are instrumental or critical for success. Err on the side of safety by not cooking too much (you can always add more but never take away) so that you get pasta in a creamy egg, bacon and cheese sauce rather than one resembling scrambled egg.

FOR ONE		FOR TWO
65 g/2½ oz	smoked pancetta or streaky bacon, finely chopped	150 g/5 oz
½	garlic clove, crushed	1
75 g/3 oz	dried spaghetti, broken in half	150 g/5 oz
15 ml/1 tbsp	grated Parmesan cheese	30 ml/2 tbsp
1	egg yolk(s)	2
	salt and freshly ground black pepper	
15 ml/1 tbsp	fresh parsley, chopped	30 ml/2 tbsp

For one

* Place the pancetta or bacon in a dish with the garlic and microwave, uncovered, on HIGH for 2¼ minutes. Remove from the microwave and drain. Set aside while cooking the spaghetti.
* Place the spaghetti in a bowl with 300 ml/½ pint boiling water and microwave, uncovered, on HIGH for 7-8 minutes until cooked 'al dente' or to your liking.
* Add the Parmesan and egg yolks with seasoning to taste to the pancetta and mix well. Add 1 tbsp of the pasta cooking water and mix well.
* Using a slotted spoon to extract the spaghetti from the residual cooking water transfer to the pancetta mixture and add the parsley. Toss the whole mixture together – the heat from the spaghetti will serve to thicken the sauce. Serve at once.

For two

* Place the pancetta or bacon in a dish with the garlic and microwave, uncovered, on HIGH for 3-3½ minutes. Remove from the microwave and drain. Set aside while cooking the spaghetti.
* Place the spaghetti in a bowl with 600 ml/1 pint boiling water and microwave, uncovered, on HIGH for 8-9 minutes until cooked 'al dente' or to your liking.
* Add the Parmesan and egg yolks with seasoning to taste to the pancetta and mix well. Add 2 tbsp of the pasta cooking water and mix well.
* Using a slotted spoon to extract the spaghetti from the residual cooking water transfer to the pancetta mixture and add the parsley. Toss the whole mixture together – the heat from the spaghetti will serve to thicken the sauce. Serve at once.

Magical stuffed green peppers

Cooking stuffed peppers in the conventional oven can be a long faff but the microwave makes light work of the job. This recipe uses peppers stuffed with minced beef or lamb, mangetout, couscous, courgette, spinach and tomatoes and is wonderfully easy to make and tastes delicious when sprinkled with crumbled feta to serve.

FOR ONE		FOR TWO
1	green pepper(s)	2
40 g/1½ oz	minced beef or lamb	75 g/3 oz
15 ml/1 tbsp	dry couscous	30 ml/2 tbsp
25 g/1 oz	courgettes, grated or finely chopped	50 g/2 oz
25 g/1 oz	mangetout, chopped	50 g/2 oz
15 ml/1 tbsp	fresh spinach leaves, chopped	30 ml/2 tbsp
40 g/1½ oz	cherry tomatoes, chopped	75 g/3 oz
½	garlic clove, chopped	1
15 ml/1 tbsp	tomato paste	30 ml/2 tbsp
1.25 ml/¼ tsp	chopped chilli (optional)	2.5 ml/½ tsp
15 ml/1 tbsp	fresh parsley, chopped	30 ml/2 tbsp
15 ml/1 tbsp	fresh coriander, chopped	30 ml/2 tbsp
7.5 ml/1½ tsp	olive oil	15 ml/1 tbsp
	salt and freshly ground black pepper	
25 g/1 oz	feta, crumbled	50 g/2 oz

For one ⸺

- Slice the top from the pepper and remove and discard the core, membrane and seeds. Place in a tight-fitting cooking dish (a large cup or mug works well) with 1 tbsp water in the base.
- To make the stuffing, mix the minced beef or lamb with the couscous, courgette, mangetout, spinach, tomatoes, garlic, tomato paste, chilli (if using), parsley, coriander and olive oil. Add 2 tbsp extra water and seasoning to taste, mixing well. Spoon the mixture into the pepper, pressing down well.
- Cover and microwave on HIGH for 8-9 minutes then check if cooked to your liking by carefully removing the cover and testing the flesh with the tip of a knife. It should be well softened but still have some bite. The timing will depend upon the size of the pepper you use. Leave to stand for 1 minute before serving, topped with the crumbled feta.

For two ⸺

- Slice the tops from the peppers and remove and discard the cores, membrane and seeds. Place in a tight-fitting cooking dish or 2 individual ones with 2 tbsp water in the base of the larger dish or 1 tbsp in each of the 2 individual ones.
- To make the stuffing, mix the minced beef or lamb with the couscous, courgette, mangetout, spinach, tomatoes, garlic, tomato paste, chilli (if using), parsley, coriander and olive oil. Add 4 tbsp extra water and seasoning to taste, mixing well. Spoon the mixture into the peppers, pressing down well.

- Cover and microwave on HIGH for 14-15 minutes then check if cooked to your liking by carefully removing the cover and testing the flesh with the tip of a knife. It should be well softened but still have some bite. The timing will depend upon the size of the peppers you use. Leave to stand for 1 minute before serving, topped with the crumbled feta.

Keep it light and simple Spanish chorizo and lentil one pot

This uncomplicated, quick-cook dish has flavours that defy the simplicity of the recipe ingredients. Spicy and robust chorizo, earthy goat's cheese and creamy, silky avocado are cooked with just a few spoonfuls of pre-cooked puy lentils to make a memorable dish with lots of complex but not competing flavours. Perfect comfort food to eat any time of the year.

FOR ONE		FOR TWO
40 g/1½ oz	chorizo, sliced	75 g/3 oz
75 g/3 oz	pre-cooked puy lentils (from a pouch)	175 g/6 oz
40 g/1½ oz	baby tomatoes, chopped	75 g/3 oz
25 g/1 oz	red pepper, chopped	50 g/2 oz
15 ml/1 tbsp	olive oil	30 ml/2 tbsp
2.5 ml/½ tsp	water	5 ml/1 tsp
30 ml/2 tbsp	fresh parsley, chopped	60 ml/4 tbsp
7.5 ml/1½ tsp	lemon juice	15 ml/1 tbsp
	salt and freshly ground black pepper	
½	small ripe avocado, cubed	1
40 g/1½ oz	goat's cheese, torn into bite-sized pieces	75 g/3 oz

For one ——

- Place the chorizo, lentils, tomatoes, pepper, olive oil and water in a dish and mix well. Cover and microwave on HIGH for 1 minute.
- Add the parsley, lemon juice and salt and pepper to taste, mixing well. Add the avocado and goat's cheese and fold in gently to serve.

For two ———

- ◆ Place the chorizo, lentils, tomatoes, pepper, olive oil and water in a dish and mix well. Cover and microwave on HIGH for 1¾-2 minutes.
- ◆ Add the parsley, lemon juice and salt and pepper to taste, mixing well. Add the avocado and goat's cheese and fold in gently to serve. Divide between 2 plates or bowls to serve.

Spanish beans

I often make and serve this dish of beans with tomatoes cooked in a smoky tomato sauce to serve with roast chicken but it will suffice alone as a main style light dish too. Add some rustic or farmhouse style bread on the side for those with larger appetites.

FOR ONE		FOR TWO
5 ml/1 tsp	olive oil	10 ml/2 tsp
40 g/1½ oz	chopped onion	75 g/3 oz
½	large garlic clove, chopped	1
1.25 ml/¼ tsp	smoked paprika	2.5 ml/½ tsp
1	bay leaf	1
150 g/5 oz	chopped fresh tomatoes	300 g/10 oz
	salt and freshly ground black pepper	
65 g/2½ oz	cooked or canned butterbeans	150 g/5 oz
25 g/1 oz	fresh spinach leaves	50 g/2 oz

For one ———

- ◆ Place the oil, onion and garlic in a dish. Cover and microwave on HIGH for 1½ minutes to soften.
- ◆ Stir in the paprika and bay leaf and microwave, uncovered, for ½ minute.
- ◆ Stir in the tomatoes and salt and pepper to taste. Cover and microwave on HIGH for 3 minutes, stirring once.
- ◆ Add the beans, mixing well, re-cover and microwave on HIGH for ½ minute.
- ◆ Add the spinach, mixing well. Re-cover and microwave on HIGH for 1 minute. Stir and leave to stand, covered for 1 minute before serving.

For two

- Place the oil, onion and garlic in a dish. Cover and microwave on HIGH for 2-3 minutes to soften.
- Stir in the paprika and bay leaf and microwave, uncovered, for 1 minute.
- Stir in the tomatoes and salt and pepper to taste. Cover and microwave on HIGH for 5 minutes, stirring once.
- Add the beans, mixing well, re-cover and microwave on HIGH for ¾ minute.
- Add the spinach, mixing well. Re-cover and microwave on HIGH for 1-1½ minutes. Stir and leave to stand, covered for 1 minute before serving.

BLTs

BLTs – American for bacon, lettuce and tomato sandwiches – are fast food favourites with a difference, as they provide a balanced nutritional meal.

FOR ONE		FOR TWO
3	rashers streaky bacon, rinded	6
2	slices wholemeal bread	4
15 ml/1 tbsp	mayonnaise	30 ml/2 tbsp
	few crisp lettuce leaves	
1	tomato(es), sliced	2

For one

- Place the bacon on a plate and cover with a sheet of absorbent kitchen towel. Microwave on HIGH for 2-3 minutes or until crisp and cooked.
- Spread one slice of bread with some of the mayonnaise. Cover with the lettuce leaves and sliced tomato.
- Top with the cooked bacon and any remaining mayonnaise. Cover with the remaining bread. Cut into triangles and serve at once.

For two

- Place the bacon on a plate and cover with a sheet of absorbent kitchen towel. Microwave on HIGH for 3½-4 minutes or until crisp and cooked.
- Spread one slice of bread with some of the mayonnaise. Cover with the lettuce leaves and sliced tomato.
- Top with the cooked bacon and any remaining mayonnaise. Cover with the remaining bread. Cut into triangles and serve at once.

Piperanda

Piperanda is rather like the classic French egg and tomato dish pipérade but is made with ham and peppers too. Serve with toast fingers or crusty Farmhouse bread wedges.

FOR ONE		FOR TWO
20 g/¾ oz	butter	40 g/1½ oz
½	small onion, peeled and chopped	1
½	small green pepper, cored, seeded and finely chopped	1
25 g/1 oz	tomatoes, chopped	50 g/2 oz
25 g/1 oz	cooked ham, chopped	50 g/2 oz
2	small eggs, beaten	4
	salt and freshly ground black pepper	
	parsley sprigs, to garnish	

For one —

* Place the butter, onion and pepper in a bowl. Cover and microwave on HIGH for 1-2 minutes, stirring once.
* Add the tomatoes, ham, eggs and salt and pepper to taste, blending well. Microwave, uncovered, on HIGH for 2-2½ minutes, stirring every ½ minute until lightly scrambled, creamy, and just set.
* Garnish with parsley sprigs and serve at once.

For two —

* Place the butter, onion and pepper in a bowl. Cover and microwave on HIGH for 2-2½ minutes, stirring once.
* Add the tomatoes, ham, eggs and salt and pepper to taste, blending well. Microwave, uncovered, on HIGH for 3-4 minutes, stirring every ½ minute until lightly scrambled, creamy, and just set.
* Garnish with parsley sprigs and serve at once.

Cook's Tip

Piperanda is a good, quick spur of the moment dish to use up leftover cooked ham.

Omelette fines herbes

Eggs cook amazingly fast in the microwave so it is important to judge the cooking time carefully when making this omelette. Err on the side of safety by undercooking and allowing a generous standing time.

FOR ONE		FOR TWO
2	eggs, beaten	4
20 ml/4 tsp	milk	45 ml/3 tbsp
	salt and freshly ground black pepper	
7 g/¼ oz	butter	15 g/½ oz
15 ml/1 tbsp	chopped fresh mixed herbs	30 ml/2 tbsp

For one ——

* Mix the eggs with the milk and salt and pepper to taste, blending well.
* Place the butter in a 15-18-cm/6-7-inch pie plate and microwave on HIGH for ½ minute. Swirl the butter over the plate to coat.
* Pour the egg mixture, cover with pierced cling film and microwave on HIGH for ¾ minute. Using a fork, move the cooked egg from the edge of the dish to the centre. Re-cover and microwave on HIGH for a further ½-1 minute. Allow to stand for 2 minutes to finish cooking.
* Loosen the omelette with a spatula, sprinkle with half of the herbs and fold in half to serve. Serve sprinkled with the remaining herbs.

For two ——

* Mix the eggs with the milk and salt and pepper to taste, blending well.
* Place the butter in a 25-cm/10-inch pie plate and microwave on HIGH for ½-¾ minute. Swirl the butter over the plate to coat.
* Pour the egg mixture, cover with pierced cling film and microwave on HIGH for 1¼-1½ minutes. Using a fork, move the cooked egg from the edge of the dish to the centre. Re-cover and microwave on HIGH for a further 1¼-1½ minutes. Allow to stand for 2 minutes to finish cooking.
* Loosen the omelette with a spatula, sprinkle with half of the herbs and fold in half to serve. Serve sprinkled with the remaining herbs.

Storecupboard standby

Another storecupboard favourite, try using grated cheese or chopped tomatoes instead of herbs.

Bacon and eggs

Crisp bacon and lightly baked eggs with a tomato garnish make delicious eating at any time of the day – breakfast, brunch, lunch or supper time. Serve with toast for a speedy feast.

FOR ONE		FOR TWO
2	rashers bacon, rinded	4
1	tomato(es), halved	2
1	egg(s)	2

For one ──

* Place the bacon on a plate and microwave on HIGH for ½ minute. Add the tomato halves, cut sides up.
* Break the egg into a small lightly greased ramekin dish or cup and puncture the yolk with the tip of a knife. Cover loosely with cling film and place on the plate.
* Microwave on HIGH for 1½ minutes then loosen the egg from the dish and slide onto the plate to serve.

For two ──

* Place the bacon on a plate and microwave on HIGH for 1 minute. Add the tomato halves, cut sides up.
* Break the eggs into two small lightly greased ramekin dishes or cups and puncture the yolks with the tip of a knife. Cover loosely with cling film and place on the plates.
* Microwave on HIGH for 2½-3 minutes then loosen the eggs from the dishes and slide onto the plates to serve.

Wholemeal muffin pizzas

Ordinary pizzas with their yeasted bread dough base really do seem too much effort for 1 or 2 – here is a good satisfying compromise, tasty home-made pizzas made with wholemeal muffins. They really do taste so good it is worth making double portions to freeze.

FOR ONE		FOR TWO
50 g/2 oz	drained canned tomatoes	100 g/4 oz
5 ml/1 tsp	tomato purée	10 ml/2 tsp
½	small onion, peeled and finely chopped	1
	pinch of dried oregano	
	pinch of dried basil	
1	wholemeal muffin(s), split	2
15 g/½ oz	sliced salami, pepperoni or garlic sausage	25 g/1 oz
2	pimiento-stuffed olives, sliced	4
40 g/1½ oz	Mozzarella cheese, grated	75 g/3 oz

For one —

* Place the tomatoes, tomato purée, onion and herbs in a bowl. Cover and microwave on HIGH for 1½-2 minutes until thick and pulpy, stirring once. Leave to cool.
* Spread the tomato mixture on top of the muffin halves. Top with the sliced sausage, olives and cheese.
* Microwave on HIGH for ¾-1¼ minutes. Serve at once.

For two —

* Place the tomatoes, tomato purée, onion and herbs in a bowl. Cover and microwave on HIGH for 3-4 minutes until thick and pulpy, stirring once. Leave to cool.
* Spread the tomato mixture on top of the muffin halves. Top with the sliced sausage, olives and cheese.
* Microwave on HIGH for 2-2½ minutes. Serve at once.

Freezability

Wholemeal muffin pizzas will freeze well for up to 2 months. Cook from frozen, 2 muffin pizza halves to serve 1 should be cooked on HIGH for 1½-2 minutes; 4 muffin pizza halves to serve 2 should be cooked on HIGH for 4-4½ minutes.

Jacket specials

Jacket potatoes make warming, highly nutritious snack and supper dishes. Use good fluffy potatoes such as King Edwards or Maris Piper for the best result.

FOR ONE		FOR TWO
1 x 225 g/8 oz	potato(es), scrubbed	2 x 225 g/8 oz
	CORNED BEEF HASH FILLING	
15 g/½ oz	savoury butter with black pepper	25 g/1 oz
25 g/1 oz	corned beef, chopped	50 g/2 oz
5 ml/1 tsp	sweet pickle	10 ml/2 tsp
	tomato and cucumber slices, to garnish	
	LEMON PRAWN FILLING	
15 g/½ oz	savoury butter with lemon and parsley	25 g/1 oz
25 g/1 oz	peeled prawns	50 g/2 oz
	lemon slices, to garnish	

For one ——

- Prick the potato and wrap in a sheet of absorbent kitchen towel. Microwave on HIGH for 4-6 minutes, turning over once. Leave to stand for 3-4 minutes to soften.
- Split the potato in half and scoop out the flesh into a bowl.
- To fill with corned beef hash mixture, mash the potato with the butter. Stir in the corned beef and pickle, blending well. Spoon back into the potato shells.
- To fill with lemon prawn mixture, mash the potato with the butter. Stir in the prawns, blending well. Spoon back into the potato shells.
- Microwave on HIGH for 1 minute to reheat. Garnish and serve at once.

For two ——

- Prick the potatoes and wrap in a sheet of absorbent kitchen towel. Microwave on HIGH for 6-8 minutes, turning over once. Leave to stand for 3-4 minutes to soften.
- Split the potatoes in half and scoop out the flesh into a bowl.
- To fill with corned beef hash mixture, mash the potatoes with the butter. Stir in the corned beef and pickle, blending well. Spoon back into the potato shells.
- To fill with lemon prawn mixture, mash the potatoes with the butter. Stir in the prawns, blending well. Spoon back into the potato shells.
- Microwave on HIGH for 1½ minutes to reheat. Garnish and serve at once.

Spicy pitta pockets

Plain or wholemeal pitta breads make ideal 'pockets' for holding savoury mixtures. In this recipe they are stuffed with a spicy curried mixture to make a sandwich with a difference.

FOR ONE		FOR TWO
75 g/3 oz	lean minced beef	175 g/6 oz
¼	small onion, peeled and chopped	½
¼	green dessert apple, cored and chopped	½
7 g/¼ oz	raisins	15 g/1 oz
1.25 ml/¼ tsp	curry powder	2.5 ml/½ tsp
	salt and freshly ground black pepper	
½	pitta bread	1
15 ml/1 tbsp	natural yoghurt	30 ml/2 tbsp
	pinch of garam masala	

For one ———

- Place the beef and onion in a bowl and microwave on HIGH for 2-3 minutes until cooked, stirring twice to break up any large lumps of mince.
- Drain off any excess fat then add the apple, raisins, curry powder and salt and pepper to taste, blending well.
- Cover and microwave on HIGH for 1-2 minutes until the apple is tender.
- Carefully cut the pitta bread in half with a sharp knife to make a pocket.
- Fill with the savoury curried beef mixture and top with the yogurt. Serve at once.

For two ———

- Place the beef and onion in a bowl and microwave on HIGH for 4-4½ minutes until cooked, stirring twice to break up any large lumps of mince.
- Drain off any excess fat then add the apple, raisins, curry powder and salt and pepper to taste, blending well.
- Cover and microwave on HIGH for 2-3 minutes until the apple is tender.
- Using a sharp knife halve the pitta breads crossways then carefully cut the halves to make two pockets.
- Fill with the savoury curried beef mixture and top with the yogurt. Serve at once.

Spicy popcorn

I have no idea how much popcorn you can consume in one sitting, but when popcorn is this easy to prepare, and can be stored away for up to a week in an airtight container, I don't think it's worth making any less than this quantity (which might well prove adequate for 4-6 servings). You have been warned though – it's very addictive!

FOR ONE, TWO OR MORE
50 g/2 oz dry popping corn kernels
15 ml/1 tbsp sesame oil
5 ml/1 tsp garlic granules
10-15 ml/2-3 tsp smoked paprika

* Place the corn kernels in a large heatproof bowl, cover and microwave on HIGH for 5-8 minutes, or until the popping stops.
* Un-cover carefully, stir in the oil, garlic granules and paprika, mixing well to distribute and coat the popped corn kernels.
* Serve warm or allow to cool then store for up to a week in an airtight container.

MAIN MEALS

Fish

Superb French style salmon and peas

This recipe is a regular repeat on my meal rota because even though it is a simple dish and easy to prepare it also tastes divine! The peas, courgettes, tomatoes and herbs all marry together superbly with the salmon (which cooks moist and never dry with microwave cooking) to make what I think is the perfect meal. I recommend it to you…

FOR ONE		FOR TWO
125 g/4 oz	frozen petit pois, defrosted	250 g/8 oz
4	cherry tomatoes, halved	8
40 g/1½ oz	courgette, chopped	75 g/3 oz
½	small garlic clove, chopped	1
15 ml/1 tbsp	fresh parsley, chopped	30 ml/2 tbsp
45 ml/3 tbsp	extra virgin olive oil	90 ml/6 tbsp
	salt and freshly ground black pepper	
1 x 90 g/3½ oz	skinless salmon fillet(s)	2 x 90 g/3½ oz
15 ml/1 tbsp	lemon juice	30 ml/2 tbsp

For one ——

- Place the petit pois, tomatoes, courgette, garlic, parsley and 2 tbsp of the olive oil in a dish. Season to taste and mix well.
- Cut the salmon fillet into about 4 pieces and add to the vegetable mixture, spooning a little over the top of the salmon. Cover and microwave on HIGH for 3-3½ minutes, until the salmon is cooked.

- Remove from the microwave and drizzle over the lemon juice and remaining olive oil to serve.

For two ——

- Place the petit pois, tomatoes, courgette, garlic, parsley and 4 tbsp of the olive oil in a dish. Season to taste and mix well.
- Cut each salmon fillet into about 4 pieces and add to the vegetable mixture, spooning a little over the top of the salmon. Cover and microwave on HIGH for 5½-6 minutes, until the fish is cooked.
- Remove from the microwave and drizzle over the lemon juice and remaining olive oil to serve.

Mardi Gras gumbo

Gumbo is a thickish stew made, in this version, with bacon, celery, onion, peppers, okra, garlic sausage, tomatoes and prawns, all flavoured with paprika and hot sauce. It isn't soupy in consistency but more of a Big-Easy style dish to stand your spoon up in. This one has all the New Orleans magical Mardi Gras tastes you would expect.

FOR ONE		FOR TWO
30 ml/2 tbsp	flour	60 ml/4 tbsp
5 ml/1 tsp	smoked or picante paprika	10 ml/2 tsp
30 ml/2 tbsp	oil	60 ml/4 tbsp
	salt and freshly ground black pepper	
1	smoked streaky bacon rasher(s), chopped	2
25 g/1 oz	onion, chopped	50 g/2 oz
½	stick of celery, chopped	1
1	garlic clove(s), crushed	2
15 ml/1 tbsp	green pepper, chopped	30 ml/2 tbsp
4	okra, coarsely chopped	8
175 ml/6 fl oz	chicken or vegetable stock	350 ml/12 fl oz
5 ml/1 tsp	fresh thyme, chopped	10 ml/2 tsp
3	baby plum tomatoes, quartered	6
40 g/1½ oz	garlic sausage, chopped	75 g/3 oz
5	king prawns	10
5 ml/1 tsp	Dijon mustard	10 ml/2 tsp
15 ml/1 tbsp	fresh parsley, chopped	30 ml/2 tbsp
15 ml/1 tbsp	lemon juice	30 ml/2 tbsp
2.5-5 ml/½-1 tsp	hot sauce	5-10 ml/1-2 tsp

For one ———

- Mix the flour with the paprika, oil and seasoning to taste in a dish. Microwave uncovered on HIGH for 2 minutes.
- Add the bacon, onion, celery, garlic, green pepper, okra, half the stock and thyme and mix well. Cover and microwave on HIGH for 4 minutes. Remove from the microwave and stir well.
- Add the tomatoes, garlic sausage, prawns, mustard, parsley, lemon juice, remaining stock and hot sauce (to taste), mixing well. Cover and microwave on HIGH for 3 minutes. Leave to stand for 3 minutes.
- Taste and adjust the seasoning if necessary before serving.

For two ———

- Mix the flour with the paprika, oil and seasoning to taste in a dish. Microwave uncovered on HIGH for 3-3½ minutes.
- Add the bacon, onion, celery, garlic, green pepper, okra, half the stock and thyme and mix well. Cover and microwave on HIGH for 6-7 minutes. Remove from the microwave and stir well.
- Add the tomatoes, garlic sausage, prawns, mustard, parsley, lemon juice, remaining stock and hot sauce (to taste), mixing well. Cover and microwave on HIGH for 4½-5 minutes. Leave to stand for 3 minutes.
- Taste and adjust the seasoning if necessary before serving.

Curried fish and new potato 'comfort blanket'

This recipe is the sole reason why I always keep a bag of fish pie mix in my freezer. The fish assortment makes it very economical to use for making fish recipes for one and two without waste. It's a 'hug of a dish' or 'comfort blanket' recipe reminiscent of fish pie but I think more luxurious. The curry powder gives a bit of a gentle kick and the addition of peas means it counts as a one pot or complete meal.

FOR ONE		FOR TWO
65 g/2½ oz	new potatoes, scrubbed and chopped	125 g/4½ oz
15 ml/1 tbsp	butter	30 ml/2 tbsp
15 ml/1 tbsp	flour	30 ml/2 tbsp
90 ml/3½ fl oz	coconut milk	180 ml/7 fl oz
5 ml/1 tsp	curry powder (strength to suit)	10 ml/2 tsp
½	garlic clove, crushed	1
5 ml/1 tsp	root ginger, grated	10 ml/2 tsp
100 g/4 oz	mixed cubed fish	225 g/8 oz
3	king prawns, halved	6
75 g/3 oz	frozen peas	175 g/6 oz
5 ml/1 tsp	fresh parsley, chopped	10 ml/2 tsp
	salt and freshly ground black pepper	

For one ——

- Place the potato and butter in a dish, cover and microwave on HIGH for 3½ minutes.
- Add the flour and a little of the milk and mix well. Gradually add the remaining milk so that you produce a mixture of smooth uncooked sauce with pieces of potato within it.
- Add the curry powder, garlic, ginger, fish, prawns, frozen peas, parsley and salt and pepper to taste, mixing well. Cover and microwave on HIGH for 2½ minutes.
- Remove from the microwave and stir well. Leave to stand, covered for 1 minute then microwave on HIGH for a further 2½ minutes until the fish and potato are cooked to serve.

For two ——

- Place the potato and butter in a dish, cover and microwave on HIGH for 5½ minutes.
- Add the flour and a little of the milk and mix well. Gradually add the remaining milk so that you produce a mixture of smooth uncooked sauce with pieces of potato within it.
- Add the curry powder, garlic, ginger, fish, prawns, frozen peas, parsley and salt and pepper to taste, mixing well. Cover and microwave on HIGH for 4½ minutes.
- Remove from the microwave and stir well. Leave to stand, covered for 1 minute then microwave on HIGH for a further 4-4½ minutes until the fish and potato are cooked to serve.

Oodles of noodles with Asian seabass

Friends say this is my speedy signature dish and one I often throw together when they visit, especially at lunchtime. It couldn't be easier to prep using dried egg noodle nests, frozen sea bass fillets (always to be found in my freezer) and whatever few green gems I find in my refrigerator vegetable drawer. It can also be made with other fish fillets like salmon but the cooking time is likely to be a little longer depending upon the thickness of the fillets.

FOR ONE		FOR TWO
1 x 50 g/2 oz	dried wholewheat noodle nests	2 x 50 g/2 oz
7.5 ml/1½ tsp	sesame oil	15 ml/1 tbsp
50 g/2 oz	pak choi, coarsely chopped	100 g/4 oz
4	mangetout, halved	8
1	mushroom(s), sliced	2
1	garlic clove(s), crushed	2
½	red chilli, seeded and chopped	1
15 ml/1 tbsp	root ginger, grated	30 ml/2 tbsp
5 ml/1 tsp	soy sauce	10 ml/2 tsp
2.5 ml/½ tsp	honey or sweet chilli sauce	5 ml/1 tsp
1 x 75 g/3 oz	sea bass fillet(s)	2 x 75 g/3 oz

For one ——

- Gently break up the noodles and place in a dish. Cover with boiling water. Microwave, uncovered, on HIGH for 5½-6 minutes, stirring halfway through the cooking, then drain well.
- Add half of the oil, pak choi, mangetout, mushrooms, garlic, three-quarters of the chilli, half of the ginger, soy sauce and honey or sweet chilli sauce to the noodles, mixing well to combine.
- Place the sea bass on top of the noodles, drizzle with the remaining oil and sprinkle with the remaining ginger. Cover and microwave on HIGH for 2½-3 minutes, then leave to stand for 2 minutes. Serve sprinkled with the remaining chilli.

For two

- Gently break up the noodles and place in a dish. Cover with boiling water. Microwave, uncovered, on HIGH for 5½-6 minutes, stirring halfway through the cooking, then drain well.
- Add half of the oil, pak choi, mangetout, mushrooms, garlic, three-quarters of the chilli, half of the ginger, soy sauce and honey or sweet chilli sauce to the noodles, mixing well to combine.
- Place the sea bass on top of the noodles, drizzle with the remaining oil and sprinkle with the remaining ginger. Cover and microwave on HIGH for 3½-4 minutes, then leave to stand for 2 minutes. Serve sprinkled with the remaining chilli.

Monkfish and prawn brochettes

Monkfish is a deep sea fish which has such an ugly head that usually only the tail is sold. Its flesh is firm, white and very succulent and makes a perfect partner to pink prawns in these delicious brochettes.

FOR ONE		FOR TWO
225 g/8 oz	monkfish tails	450 g/1 lb
4	large Mediterranean prawns, peeled	8
2	bay leaves	4
15 ml/1 tbsp	olive oil	30 ml/2 tbsp
	freshly ground white pepper	
1	recipe hot Hollandaise Sauce, to serve (see page 153)	1

For one

- Skin the monkfish, then remove the flesh from either side of the central bone. Cut into bite-sized chunks.
- Thread onto a short wooden skewer, alternating with the prawns and bay leaves. Brush with the olive oil and season with pepper to taste.
- Cover loosely with cling film and microwave on HIGH for 2½-3 minutes until the monkfish is opaque and flakes easily when tested with a fork. Serve with hot Hollandaise sauce (see page 153).

For two ——

* Skin the monkfish, then remove the flesh from either side of the central bone. Cut into bite-sized chunks.
* Thread onto short wooden skewers, alternating with the prawns and bay leaves. Brush with the olive oil and season with pepper to taste.
* Cover loosely with cling film and microwave on HIGH for 5-7 minutes until the monkfish is opaque and flakes easily when tested with a fork. Serve with hot Hollandaise sauce (see page 153).

Fragrant seafood paella

This Spanish speciality relies upon saffron strands for its fragrant aroma and flavour. If unavailable use a little ground turmeric instead to achieve the same golden yellow rice but not the same flavour.

FOR ONE		FOR TWO
7.5 ml/1½ tsp	olive oil	15 ml/1 tbsp
½	small onion, peeled and chopped	1
½	garlic clove, peeled and chopped	1
75 g/3 oz	long grain rice	175 g/6 oz
175 ml/6 oz	boiling chicken stock	350 ml/12 fl oz
	pinch of saffron strands	
	salt and freshly ground black pepper	
25 g/1 oz	frozen peas	50 g/2 oz
5	mussels cooked then left on their half shells	10
50 g/2 oz	cooked chicken, skinned and chopped	100 g/4 oz
4	whole prawns	8
25 g/1 oz	hot spicy sausage, diced	50 g/2 oz

For one ——

* Place the oil, onion and garlic in a large bowl. Cover and microwave on HIGH for 1½-2 minutes.
* Stir in the rice, stock, saffron strands and salt and pepper to taste, blending well. Cover and microwave on HIGH for 3 minutes. Reduce the power setting and microwave on MEDIUM for a further 10 minutes, stirring twice. Leave to stand, covered, for 5 minutes or until the rice is tender and the liquid absorbed.
* Add the peas, mussels, chicken, prawns and sausage, tossing lightly to mix. Cover and microwave on HIGH for 2-3 minutes to reheat. Serve at once.

For two —

- Place the oil, onion and garlic in a large bowl. Cover and microwave on HIGH for 3-4 minutes.
- Stir in the rice, stock, saffron strands and salt and pepper to taste, blending well. Cover and microwave on HIGH for 3 minutes. Reduce the power setting and microwave on MEDIUM for a further 10 minutes, stirring twice. Leave to stand, covered, for 5 minutes or until the rice is tender and the liquid absorbed.
- Add the peas, mussels, chicken, prawns and sausage, tossing lightly to mix. Cover and microwave on HIGH for 3-4 minutes to reheat. Serve at once.

Chive fish bake

Quick mid-week meals need not be complicated or repetitive – here is a deliciously easy recipe which is perfect for a weekday supper.

FOR ONE		FOR TWO
1 x 175 g/6 oz	piece(s) of cod or haddock fillet(s)	2 x 175 g/6 oz
5 ml/1 tsp	chive mustard	10 ml/2 tsp
25 g/1 oz	Cheddar cheese, grated	50 g/2 oz
1	tomato(es), sliced	2

For one —

- Place the fish in a small shallow dish. Spread with the chive mustard and sprinkle with the cheese. Arrange the tomato slices over the top.
- Cover and microwave on HIGH for 3-4 minutes or until the fish is opaque and flakes easily when tested with a fork.
- Serve at once with vegetables in season.

For two —

- Place the fish in a shallow dish. Spread with the chive mustard and sprinkle with the cheese. Arrange the tomato slices over the top.
- Cover and microwave on HIGH for 5-6 minutes or until the fish is opaque and flakes easily when tested with a fork.
- Serve at once with vegetables in season.

Seafood and fish pie

Chunks of white fish and prawns topped with fluffy potato make a welcome change to the usual mid-week cottage pie.

FOR ONE		FOR TWO
100 g/4 oz	cooked white fish, flaked into chunks	225 g/8 oz
50 g/2 oz	peeled prawns	100 g/4 oz
150 ml/¼ pint	hot Basic White or Parsley Sauce (see page 149/150)	300 ml/½ pint
200 g/7 oz	potatoes, peeled and cubed	400 g/14 oz
15 ml/ 1 tbsp	water	30 ml/2 tbsp
15 g/½ oz	butter	25 g/1 oz
	salt and freshly ground black pepper	

For one —

* Mix the fish with the prawns and sauce in a small ovenproof dish.
* Place the potato and water in a bowl. Cover and microwave on HIGH for 4-5 minutes until tender. Drain and mash with the butter and salt and pepper to taste. Pipe or spoon over the fish mixture to cover.
* Microwave on HIGH for 2 minutes to reheat then brown under a preheated grill, if liked.

For two —

* Mix the fish with the prawns and sauce in an ovenproof dish.
* Place the potato and water in a bowl. Cover and microwave on HIGH for 8-10 minutes until tender. Drain and mash with the butter and salt and pepper to taste. Pipe or spoon over the fish mixture to cover.
* Microwave on HIGH for 4 minutes to reheat then brown under a preheated grill, if liked.

Cod Créole

This interesting pepper and tomato sauce makes ordinary cod something special. Serve with boiled rice.

FOR ONE		FOR TWO
7 g/¼ oz	butter	15 g/½ oz
½	small onion, peeled and finely chopped	1
½	small green pepper, cored, seeded and sliced	1
2.5 ml/½ tsp	flour	5 ml/1 tsp
½ x 225 g/8 oz	can tomatoes, drained	1 x 225 g/8 oz
15 ml/1 tbsp	tomato purée	30 ml/2 tbsp
	dash of hot pepper sauce	
30 ml/2 tbsp	dry white wine or fish stock	60 ml/4 tbsp
	salt	
100 g/4 oz	cod fillet, skinned and cut into bite-sized pieces	225 g/8 oz
	chopped fresh parsley, to garnish	

For one ——

- Place the butter, onion and pepper in a bowl. Cover and microwave on HIGH for 2 minutes. Stir in the flour, blending well.
- Add the tomatoes, tomato purée, hot pepper sauce, wine or stock and salt to taste, blending well. Microwave on HIGH for 2-2½ minutes, stirring once.
- Add the cod, cover and microwave on HIGH for a further 2-3 minutes or until the fish is cooked. Garnish with chopped parsley and serve at once.

For two ——

- Place the butter, onion and pepper in a bowl. Cover and microwave on HIGH for 4 minutes. Stir in the flour, blending well.
- Add the tomatoes, tomato purée, hot pepper sauce, wine or stock and salt to taste, blending well. Microwave on HIGH for 4 minutes, stirring once.
- Add the cod, cover and microwave on HIGH for a further 3-5 minutes or until the fish is cooked. Garnish with chopped parsley and serve at once.

Creamy seafood pasta

Almost any kind of cooked seafood may be used in this recipe; the quantities below give a good variety of textures, colours and flavours.

FOR ONE		FOR TWO
50 g/2 oz	multi-coloured dried pasta twists or shells	100 g/4 oz
300 ml/½ pint	boiling fish or chicken stock	450 ml/¾ pint
25 g/1 oz	canned tuna, flaked	50 g/2 oz
25 g/1 oz	large peeled prawns	50 g/2 oz
25 g/1 oz	fresh, frozen or canned mussels	50 g/2 oz
15 g/½ oz	fresh, frozen or canned crabmeat, flaked	25 g/1 oz
SAUCE		
7 g/¼ oz	butter	15 g/½ oz
25 ml/1 fl oz	double cream	50 ml/2 fl oz
25 g/1 oz	cream cheese	50 g/2 oz
25 g/1 oz	mild herb-flavoured cream cheese	50 g/2 oz
	pinch of finely chopped fresh mixed herbs	
	salt and freshly ground black pepper	

For one ——

- Place the pasta in a deep bowl with the boiling stock. Cover and microwave on HIGH for 12-14 minutes then allow to stand for 5-10 minutes until tender.
- Meanwhile mix the tuna with the prawns, mussels and crabmeat, blending well.
- To make the sauce, place the butter and cream in a bowl. Microwave on HIGH for ¼-½ minute.
- Gradually beat in the cream cheeses, the herbs and salt and pepper to taste.
- Reduce the power setting to MEDIUM and microwave for 1 minute until hot, stirring once.
- To serve, drain the pasta and toss with the fish mixture. Cover and microwave on HIGH for ½-1 minute to reheat.
- Pour the sauce over the pasta and toss gently to mix. Serve at once with a crisp green salad, if liked.

For two ——

- Place the pasta in a deep bowl with the boiling stock. Cover and microwave on HIGH for 12-14 minutes then allow to stand for 5-10 minutes until tender.
- Meanwhile mix the tuna with the prawns, mussels and crabmeat, blending well.
- To make the sauce, place the butter and cream in a bowl. Microwave on HIGH for ½-¾ minute.

- Gradually beat in the cream cheeses, the herbs and salt and pepper to taste.
- Reduce the power setting to MEDIUM and microwave for 2 minutes until hot, stirring once.
- To serve, drain the pasta and toss with the fish mixture. Cover and microwave on HIGH for 1-1½ minutes to reheat.
- Pour the sauce over the pasta and toss gently to mix. Serve at once with a crisp green salad, if liked.

Poached salmon with cucumber herb sauce

Pink, moist and succulent, fresh salmon may seem extravagant when cooking for 4, but costs little more than meat for a single or double serving these days.

FOR ONE		FOR TWO
1 x 175 g/6 oz	salmon steaks, about 2.5 cm/1 inch thick	2 x 175 g/6 oz
7 g/¼ oz	butter	15 g/½ oz
30 ml/2 tbsp	dry vermouth	60 ml/4 tbsp
	freshly ground black pepper	
	SAUCE	
40 g/1½ oz	cucumber, cut into thin strips	75 g/3 oz
7 g/¼ oz	butter	15 g/½ oz
5 ml/1 tsp	snipped chives	10 ml/2 tsp
5 ml/1 tsp	chopped fresh tarragon or dill	10 ml/2 tsp
5 ml/1 tsp	flour	10 ml/2 tsp
5 ml/1 tsp	lemon juice	10 ml/2 tsp
5 ml/1 tsp	cream cheese	10 ml/2 tsp
10 ml/2 tsp	double cream	20 ml/4 tsp
	salt and freshly ground black pepper	
	lemon slices and fresh tarragon or dill, to garnish	

For one ———

- Place the salmon steak in a small greased shallow dish. Dot with the butter, pour over the vermouth and sprinkle with black pepper. Cover with cling film and microwave on HIGH for 1½ minutes or until the fish flakes easily when tested with a fork. Transfer the salmon to a warmed serving dish. Reserve the cooking juices for the sauce.

- To make the sauce, place the cucumber and butter in a small bowl. Cover and microwave on HIGH for 1½ minutes, stirring once. Add the herbs, blending well. Cover and microwave on HIGH for ½ minute.
- Add the flour, blending well. Gradually add the reserved cooking juices, lemon juice and the cream cheese, beating well to blend. Microwave on HIGH for 1 minute, stirring once until smooth and thickened. Stir in the cream and salt and pepper to taste.
- Spoon the sauce over the salmon. Garnish with lemon slices and sprigs of tarragon or dill and serve at once.

For two

- Place the salmon steaks in a greased shallow dish. Dot with the butter, pour over the vermouth and sprinkle with black pepper. Cover with cling film and microwave on HIGH for 2-2½ minutes or until the fish flakes easily when tested with a fork. Transfer the salmon to a warmed serving dish. Reserve the cooking juices for the sauce.
- To make the sauce, place the cucumber and butter in a small bowl. Cover and microwave on HIGH for 2-2½ minutes, stirring once. Add the herbs, blending well. Cover and microwave on HIGH for 1 minute.
- Add the flour, blending well. Gradually add the reserved cooking juices, lemon juice and the cream cheese, beating well to blend. Microwave on HIGH for 1½ minutes, stirring once until smooth and thickened. Stir in the cream and salt and pepper to taste.
- Spoon the sauce over the salmon. Garnish with lemon slices and sprigs of tarragon or dill and serve at once.

Cook's tip

Poached Salmon with Cucumber Herb Sauce is delicious served with Mangetout à la Française (see page 131) and Fantail Lemon Courgettes (see page 127).

Kedgeree

This Victorian classic has recently become popular in fashionable restaurants countrywide. Serve as a supper dish or as part of a weekend brunch.

FOR ONE		FOR TWO
50 g/2 oz	long-grain rice	100 g/4 oz
300 ml/½ pint	boiling water	450 ml/¾ pint
	salt and freshly ground black pepper	
15 g/½ oz	butter	25 g/1 oz
2.5 ml/½ tsp	finely grated lemon rind	5 ml/1 tsp
100 g/4 oz	cooked, smoked haddock, skinned, boned and flaked	200 g/8 oz
7.5 ml/1½ tsp	chopped fresh parsley	15 ml/1 tbsp
	pinch of ground nutmeg	
10 ml/2 tsp	double cream	20 ml/4 tsp
½	small hard-boiled egg, shelled and chopped	1

For one

* Place the rice and water and salt to taste in a bowl. Cover and microwave on HIGH for 3 minutes. Reduce the power setting and microwave on MEDIUM for 12 minutes, stirring once. Leave to stand for 5 minutes then drain if necessary.
* Place the butter and lemon rind in a bowl and microwave on HIGH for ½ minute to melt. Add the rice, haddock, parsley and salt, pepper and nutmeg to taste, blending well.
* Fold in the cream and hard-boiled egg and microwave on HIGH for ½-¾ minute to reheat.

For two

* Place the rice and water and salt to taste in a bowl. Cover and microwave on HIGH for 3 minutes. Reduce the power setting and microwave on MEDIUM for 12 minutes, stirring once. Leave to stand for 5 minutes then drain if necessary.
* Place the butter and lemon rind in a bowl and microwave on HIGH for 1 minute to melt. Add the rice, haddock, parsley and salt, pepper and nutmeg to taste, blending well.
* Fold in the cream and hard-boiled egg and microwave on HIGH for ¾-1 minute to reheat.

Tuna stuffed peppers

The secret in cooking these peppers so that they remain colourful yet tender is to par-cook them before stuffing.

FOR ONE		FOR TWO
1	red, green or yellow pepper(s)	2
15 ml/1 tbsp	water	15 ml/1 tbsp
1	small tomato(es), skinned, seeded and chopped	2
½	small onion, peeled and chopped	1
15 ml/1 tbsp	fresh white breadcrumbs	30 ml/2 tbsp
50 g/2 oz	canned tuna fish, drained and flaked	100 g/4 oz
7.5 ml/1½ tsp	tomato sauce or ketchup	15 ml/1 tbsp
	salt and freshly ground black pepper	
	knob of butter	

For one ——

- Cut the top off the pepper and remove and discard the core and seeds. Place in a dish with the water. Cover and microwave on HIGH for 1½ minutes. Turn the pepper over and microwave on HIGH for a further 1½ minutes.
- Meanwhile mix the tomato with the onion, breadcrumbs, tuna fish, tomato sauce and salt and pepper to taste, blending well. Spoon into the pepper.
- Dot with a knob of butter. Cover and microwave on HIGH for 2 minutes. Leave to stand, covered, for 3 minutes before serving.

For two ——

- Cut the top off the peppers and remove and discard the core and seeds. Place in a dish with the water. Cover and microwave on HIGH for 2½-3 minutes. Turn the peppers over and microwave on HIGH for a further 2½-3 minutes.
- Meanwhile mix the tomatoes with the onion, breadcrumbs, tuna fish, tomato sauce and salt and pepper to taste, blending well. Spoon into the peppers.
- Dot with a knob of butter. Cover and microwave on HIGH for 4 minutes. Leave to stand, covered, for 3 minutes before serving.

Cook's tip

Try substituting canned salmon or crabmeat for tuna, or use cooked leftover chicken for a change.

Trout with almonds

Another classic dish made easy with the microwave. Serve with new potatoes and green beans to make a complete meal.

FOR ONE		FOR TWO
7.5 ml/1½ tsp	lemon juice	15 ml/1 tbsp
25 g/1 oz	flaked almonds	50 g/2 oz
15 g/½ oz	butter	25 g/1 oz
1	medium trout(s), cleaned and gutted	2
	lemon slices and parsley sprigs, to garnish	

For one ——

- Place the lemon juice, almonds and butter in a shallow dish. Microwave on HIGH for 1 minute to melt the butter.
- Add the trout and turn on all sides to coat evenly with the buttered almond mixture. Cover and microwave on HIGH for 2-3 minutes, turning over once.
- Allow to stand for 3 minutes or until the fish flakes easily when tested with a fork. Garnish with lemon slices and parsley sprigs and serve at once.

For two ——

- Place the lemon juice, almonds and butter in a shallow dish. Microwave on HIGH for 2 minutes to melt the butter.
- Add the trout and turn on all sides to coat evenly with the buttered almond mixture. Cover and microwave on HIGH for 5 minutes, turning over once.
- Allow to stand for 3 minutes or until the fish flakes easily when tested with a fork. Garnish with lemon slices and parsley sprigs and serve at once.

Codswallop

A tasty fish dish whose reputation after sampling surpasses its unfortunate name!

FOR ONE		FOR TWO
1 x 175 g/6 oz	white fish fillet(s)	2 x 175 g/6 oz
½	small onion, peeled and sliced	1
1	tomato(es), thinly sliced	2
50 g/2 oz	sweetcorn kernels	100 g/4 oz
30 ml/2 tbsp	dry cider	60 ml/4 tbsp
	pinch of dried mixed herbs	
	salt and freshly ground black pepper	
15 ml/1 tbsp	brown breadcrumbs	30 ml/2 tbsp
15 g/½ oz	Cheddar cheese, grated	25 g/1 oz

For one —

- Place the fish in a small gratin dish and cover with the onion, tomatoes and corn.
- Pour over the cider and sprinkle with the herbs and salt and pepper to taste. Cover and microwave on HIGH for 3-4 minutes. Reduce the power setting to MEDIUM and cook for 3 minutes. Leave to stand for 5 minutes or until tender.
- Sprinkle with the breadcrumbs and cheese. Brown under a preheated grill and serve at once.

For two —

- Place the fish in a gratin dish and cover with the onion, tomatoes and corn.
- Pour over the cider and sprinkle with the herbs and salt and pepper to taste. Cover and microwave on HIGH for 6 minutes. Reduce the power setting to MEDIUM and cook for 5 minutes. Leave to stand for 5 minutes or until tender.
- Sprinkle with the breadcrumbs and cheese. Brown under a preheated grill and serve at once.

Meat

Hurry satay lamb curry

This really is a hurry curry where straight-to-wok noodles short circuit the usual lengthy prep of making a pretty authentic lamb satay curry that can be ready to eat in about 8 minutes. Beansprouts and crushed peanuts add crunch, coconut milk and peanut butter bring creamy flavour, and lamb, with satay seasonings brings soul to the table in record time.

FOR ONE		FOR TWO
½ x 150 g/5 oz packet	straight to wok noodles	1 x 150 g/5 oz packet
10 ml/2 tsp	vegetable oil	20 ml/4 tsp
2.5 ml/½ tsp	sesame oil	5 ml/1 tsp
25 g/1 oz	onions, sliced	50 g/2 oz
1	garlic clove(s), chopped	2
40 g/1½ oz	runner or fine beans, thinly sliced	75 g/3 oz
25 g/1 oz	beansprouts	50 g/2 oz
100 ml/3½ fl oz	coconut milk	200 ml/7 fl oz
30 ml/2 tbsp	peanut butter	60 ml/4 tbsp
5 ml/1 tsp	fish sauce	10 ml/2 tsp
2.5 ml/½ tsp	dark soy sauce	5 ml/1 tsp
1.25 ml/¼ tsp	sugar	2.5 ml/½ tsp
	salt and freshly ground black pepper	
75 g/3 oz	lamb steak, finely sliced	175 g/6 oz
5 ml/1 tsp	roasted peanuts, crushed	10 ml/2 tsp

For one ——

* Remove the noodles from the packet and separate by gently pulling apart. Place in a dish with 1½ tsp of the vegetable oil, sesame oil, onions, garlic, beans and beansprouts, mixing well. Microwave, uncovered, on HIGH for 2 minutes.
* Add the coconut milk, peanut butter, fish sauce, soy sauce, sugar and salt and pepper to taste, mixing well. Place the sliced lamb pieces on top and drizzle with the remaining oil. Microwave, uncovered, on HIGH for 1½ minutes, stir well then microwave, uncovered, on HIGH for a further 1-1½ minutes.
* Cover and leave to stand for 3 minutes, then stir to serve topped with the crushed roasted peanuts.

For two ——

* Remove the noodles from the packet and separate by gently pulling apart. Place in a dish with 3 tsp of the vegetable oil, sesame oil, onions, garlic, beans and beansprouts, mixing well. Microwave, uncovered, on HIGH for 3½ minutes.
* Add the coconut milk, peanut butter, fish sauce, soy sauce, sugar and salt and pepper to taste, mixing well. Place the sliced lamb pieces on top and drizzle with the remaining oil. Microwave, uncovered, on HIGH for 2½ minutes, stir well then microwave, uncovered, on HIGH for a further 1½-2 minutes.
* Cover and leave to stand for 3 minutes, then stir to serve topped with the crushed roasted peanuts.

Sweet potato shepherd's pie

This is a typical lamb-based Shepherd's Pie but with a fluffy topping of sweet potato rather than the conventional potato kind. It doesn't need baking or grilling to give a golden crown so you save loads of time when preparing but not a bit of the flavour or golden finish.

FOR ONE		FOR TWO
150 g/5 oz	sweet potatoes, peeled and finely chopped	300 g/10 oz
7.5 ml/1½ tsp	butter	15 ml/1 tbsp
	salt and freshly ground black pepper	
15 ml/1 tbsp	oil	30 ml/2 tbsp
15 ml/1 tbsp	onion, chopped	30 ml/2 tbsp
1	garlic clove(s), crushed	2
1	carrot(s), peeled and finely chopped	2
2.5 ml/½ tsp	chilli, chopped (optional)	5 ml/1 tsp
75 g/3 oz	minced lamb	150 g/6 oz
50 g/2 oz	frozen peas	100 g/4 oz
2.5 ml/½ tsp	dried mixed herbs	5 ml/1 tsp
2.5 ml/½ tsp	ground allspice	5 ml/1 tsp
5 ml/1 tsp	brown sugar	10 ml/2 tsp
5 ml/1 tsp	vinegar	10 ml/2 tsp
5 ml/1 tsp	tomato paste	10 ml/2 tsp
2.5 ml/½ tsp	ground cinnamon	5 ml/1 tsp
15 ml/1 tbsp	gravy granules	30 ml/2 tbsp
5 ml/1 tsp	fresh mint, chopped	10 ml/2 tsp

For one ——

+ Make the sweet potato topping first by placing the sweet potato and 75 ml/3 fl oz water in a dish. Cover and microwave on HIGH for 5-6 minutes until cooked and soft. Drain well, add the butter and seasoning to taste and mash with a fork to a rough consistency. Keep warm.
+ Place the oil, onion, garlic, carrot and chilli if using in a dish. Microwave, uncovered, on HIGH for 3½-4 minutes until softened.
+ Add the lamb, peas, dried herbs, allspice, sugar, vinegar, tomato paste, cinnamon and gravy granules, 2 tbsp water and salt and pepper to taste, mixing well. Microwave, uncovered, on HIGH for 3-4 minutes.
+ Remove from the microwave, stir well and leave to stand for 1 minute. Stir in the chopped mint then top with the prepared sweet potato to serve.

For two —

* Make the sweet potato topping first by placing the sweet potato and 175 ml/6 fl oz water in a dish. Cover and microwave on HIGH for 7 minutes until cooked and soft. Drain well, add the butter and seasoning to taste and mash with a fork to a rough consistency. Keep warm.
* Place the oil, onion, garlic, carrot and chilli if using in a dish. Microwave, uncovered, on HIGH for 4-5 minutes until softened.
* Add the lamb, peas, dried herbs, allspice, sugar, vinegar, tomato paste, cinnamon and gravy granules, 2 tbsp water and salt and pepper to taste, mixing well. Microwave, uncovered, on HIGH for 5 minutes.
* Remove from the microwave, stir well and leave to stand for 1 minute. Stir in the chopped mint then top with the prepared sweet potato to serve.

Quick time North African tagine

I know you shouldn't profess to having favourites in a recipe collection because they are often only fleeting 'faves' depending upon season – but this tagine is one that is very dear to my taste buds and I don't tire of it regardless of the time of year it's eaten. I don't know if it's the aromatic lamb mixture, contrast of textures it has, or its colourful nature – just give me more of it!

FOR ONE		FOR TWO
50 g/2 oz	aubergine, chopped	100 g/4 oz
30 ml/2 tbsp	onion, chopped	60 ml/4 tbsp
1	garlic clove(s), crushed	2
45 ml/3 tbsp	olive oil	90 ml/6 tbsp
15 ml/1 tbsp	tomato paste	30 ml/2 tbsp
2.5 ml/½ tsp	ground cumin	5 ml/1 tsp
2.5 ml/½ tsp	ground cinnamon	5 ml/1 tsp
2.5 ml/½ tsp	smoked paprika	5 ml/1 tsp
75 ml/3 fl oz	lamb or vegetable stock	175 ml/6 fl oz
100 g/4 oz	cooked or canned chickpeas	225 g/8 oz
	salt and freshly ground black pepper	
25 g/1 oz	dried dates, sliced	50 g/2 oz
15 ml/1 tbsp	flaked almonds	30 ml/2 tbsp
75 g/3 oz	lean lamb, chopped into bite-sized pieces	175 g/6 oz
15 ml/1 tbsp	pomegranate seeds	30 ml/2 tbsp
	coriander sprigs to garnish	

For one ⸺

- Place the aubergine, onion, garlic, 2 tbsp of the oil, tomato paste, cumin, cinnamon, smoked paprika and 25 ml/1 fl oz of the stock in a dish, mixing well. Cover and microwave on HIGH for 3 minutes.
- Remove from the microwave, stir well then add the chickpeas, remaining stock and salt and pepper to taste. Re-cover and microwave on HIGH for 4 minutes.
- Remove from the microwave and stir in the dates and almonds. Place the lamb pieces on top of the mixture, drizzle over the remaining oil and season again generously. Microwave, uncovered, on HIGH for 1-1½ minutes, then fold the lamb into the vegetable mixture. Cover and leave to stand for 2 minutes. Serve sprinkled with the pomegranate seeds and garnished with coriander sprigs.

For two ⸺

- Place the aubergine, onion, garlic, 4 tbsp of the oil, tomato paste, cumin, cinnamon, smoked paprika and 50 ml/2 fl oz of the stock in a dish, mixing well. Cover and microwave on HIGH for 5 minutes.
- Remove from the microwave, stir well then add the chickpeas, remaining stock and salt and pepper to taste. Re-cover and microwave on HIGH for 6-7 minutes.
- Remove from the microwave and stir in the dates and almonds. Place the lamb pieces on top of the mixture, drizzle over the remaining oil and season again generously. Microwave, uncovered, on HIGH for 2-3 minutes, then fold the lamb into the vegetable mixture. Cover and leave to stand for 2 minutes. Serve sprinkled with the pomegranate seeds and garnished with coriander sprigs.

Stir fry lamb and courgettes

A light dish to make in spring when English lamb and courgettes are at their best; and at only 160 calories per portion it makes a good meal to include in a calorie-controlled diet.

FOR ONE		FOR TWO
10 ml/2 tsp	oil	15 ml/1 tbsp
100 g/4 oz	lamb leg steaks, cut into thin strips	225 g/8 oz
100 g/4 oz	courgettes, thinly sliced	225 g/8 oz
4	spring onions, trimmed and sliced	8
½	garlic clove, peeled and crushed	1
15 ml/1 tbsp	dry sherry	30 ml/2 tbsp
	salt and freshly ground black pepper	

For one ⸺

- Preheat a browning dish on HIGH for 8 minutes or according to the manufacturer's instructions. Add the oil and microwave on HIGH for 1 minute.
- Add the lamb and turn in the hot oil to brown evenly on all sides. Microwave on HIGH for 1½ minutes, stirring once.
- Add the courgettes, spring onions and garlic, blending well, and microwave on HIGH for 2 minutes, stirring once.
- Add the sherry and salt and pepper to taste, blending well. Microwave on HIGH for a further 1 minute. Serve at once with rice or noodles.

For two ⸺

- Preheat a browning dish on HIGH for 8 minutes or according to the manufacturer's instructions. Add the oil and microwave on HIGH for 1 minute.
- Add the lamb and turn in the hot oil to brown evenly on all sides. Microwave on HIGH for 3 minutes, stirring once.
- Add the courgettes, spring onions and garlic, blending well, and microwave on HIGH for 3-3½ minutes, stirring once.
- Add the sherry and salt and pepper to taste, blending well. Microwave on HIGH for a further 1½-2 minutes. Serve at once with rice or noodles.

Barbecued lamb with apricots

Plain lamb cutlets are made special and given extra flavour in this recipe by cooking with dried apricots, onion, ginger, cucumber and spicy barbecue beans.

FOR ONE		FOR TWO
7.5 ml/1½ tsp	oil	15 ml/1 tbsp
½	small onion, peeled and thinly sliced	1
2	small lamb cutlets, trimmed	4
	pinch of ground ginger	
100 g/4 oz	canned barbecued beans	225 g/8 oz
25 g/1 oz	dried apricots, soaked overnight in cold water	50 g/2 oz
⅛	cucumber, seeded and cut into thin strips	¼
	salt and freshly ground black pepper	

For one ——

- Preheat a browning dish on HIGH for 8 minutes or according to the manufacturer's instructions.
- Add the oil and microwave on HIGH for a further 1 minute.
- Add the onion, lamb cutlets and ginger and turn in the hot oil to brown evenly on all sides. Microwave on HIGH for 2-3 minutes, turning over once.
- Add the beans, drained apricots, cucumber and salt and pepper to taste, blending well. Microwave on HIGH for 1½-2 minutes until hot and bubbling.
- Serve at once with jacket baked potatoes.

For two ——

- Preheat a browning dish on HIGH for 8 minutes or according to the manufacturer's instructions.
- Add the oil and microwave on HIGH for a further 1 minute.
- Add the onion, lamb cutlets and ginger and turn in the hot oil to brown evenly on all sides. Microwave on HIGH for 3-3½ minutes, turning over once.
- Add the beans, drained apricots, cucumber and salt and pepper to taste, blending well. Microwave on HIGH for 2½-3 minutes until hot and bubbling.
- Serve at once with jacket baked potatoes.

Mustard pork Stroganoff

Stroganoff is a dish that originates from Russia and is traditionally made with beef. The distinctive flavour of this dish results from the combination of the paprika and soured cream. Here is a quick version using pork fillet.

FOR ONE		FOR TWO
225 g/8 oz	pork fillet	450 g/1 lb
15 g/½ oz	butter	25 g/1 oz
½	small onion, peeled and chopped	1
7.5 ml/1½ tsp	sweet paprika	15 ml/1 tbsp
2.5 ml/½ tsp	mustard powder	5 ml/1 tsp
45 ml/3 tbsp	hot chicken stock	75 ml/5 tbsp
7.5 ml/1½ tsp	tomato purée	15 ml/1 tbsp
45 ml/ 3 tbsp	soured cream	75 ml/5 tbsp
	salt and freshly ground black pepper	

For one

- Slice the pork into thin strips or medallions. Preheat a browning dish on HIGH for 8 minutes or according to the manufacturer's instructions.
- Add the butter and swirl quickly to melt. Add the pork and turn quickly in the hot butter to brown evenly on all sides.
- Add the onion and microwave on HIGH for 3 minutes, stirring once.
- Add the paprika, mustard, stock and tomato purée, blending well. Cover and microwave on HIGH for 1-1½ minutes.
- Stir in the soured cream and salt and pepper to taste. Serve hot with buttered tagliatelle.

For two

- Slice the pork into thin strips or medallions. Preheat a browning dish on HIGH for 8 minutes or according to the manufacturer's instructions.
- Add the butter and swirl quickly to melt. Add the pork and turn quickly in the hot butter to brown evenly on all sides.
- Add the onion and microwave on HIGH for 5 minutes, stirring once.
- Add the paprika, mustard, stock and tomato purée, blending well. Cover and microwave on HIGH for 2½ minutes.
- Stir in the soured cream and salt and pepper to taste. Serve hot with buttered tagliatelle.

Sweet and sour pork balls

Red, yellow and green peppers add colour and charm to this simple dish. Serve with boiled rice, ribbon noodles or a crisp seasonal salad.

FOR ONE		FOR TWO
175 g/6 oz	minced raw pork	350 g/12 oz
½	small onion, peeled and chopped	1
	salt and freshly ground black pepper	
10 ml/2 tsp	oil	15 ml/1 tbsp
¼	red pepper, cored, seeded and sliced	½
¼	yellow pepper, cored, seeded and sliced	½
¼	green pepper, cored, seeded and sliced	½
7.5 ml/1½ tsp	red wine vinegar	15 ml/1 tbsp
7.5 ml/1½ tsp	demerara sugar	15 ml/1 tbsp
2.5 ml/½ tsp	soy sauce	5 ml/1 tsp
37.5 ml/2½ tbsp	unsweetened orange juice	75 ml/5 tbsp
37.5 ml/2½ tbsp	chicken stock	75 ml/5 tbsp
	pinch of ground ginger	
	pinch of Chinese 5 spice powder	
5 ml/1 tsp	cornflour	10 ml/2 tsp

For one —

- Mix the pork with the onion and salt and pepper to taste, blending well. Divide the mixture into 4 and shape into meatballs.
- Preheat a browning dish on HIGH for 8 minutes or according to the manufacturer's instructions.
- Add the oil to the browning dish and swirl to coat the base of the dish. Microwave on HIGH for a further 1 minute.
- Add the meatballs and turn in the hot oil to brown evenly. Microwave on HIGH for 2½-3 minutes, turning over once.
- Remove the meatballs with a slotted spoon and set aside. Add the peppers to the juices in the dish, blending well. Cover and microwave on HIGH for 2½-3 minutes, stirring once.
- Add the vinegar, sugar, soy sauce, orange juice, stock, ginger, Chinese 5 spice powder and salt and pepper to taste, blending well. Microwave on HIGH for 1-1½ minutes.

- Mix the cornflour to a smooth paste with a little water. Stir into the pepper mixture, blending well. Microwave on HIGH for ½-¾ minute, stirring twice.
- Return the meatballs to the dish and baste with the sauce. Microwave on HIGH for 1-1½ minutes. Serve at once.

For two

- Mix the pork with the onion and salt and pepper to taste, blending well. Divide the mixture into 8 and shape into meatballs.
- Preheat a browning dish on HIGH for 8 minutes or according to the manufacturer's instructions.
- Add the oil to the browning dish and swirl to coat the base of the dish. Microwave on HIGH for a further 1 minute.
- Add the meatballs and turn in the hot oil to brown evenly. Microwave on HIGH for 4 minutes, turning over once.
- Remove the meatballs with a slotted spoon and set aside. Add the peppers to the juices in the dish, blending well. Cover and microwave on HIGH for 4 minutes, stirring once.
- Add the vinegar, sugar, soy sauce, orange juice, stock, ginger, Chinese 5 spice powder and salt and pepper to taste, blending well. Microwave on HIGH for 2 minutes.
- Mix the cornflour to a smooth paste with a little water. Stir into the pepper mixture, blending well. Microwave on HIGH for 1 minute, stirring twice.
- Return the meatballs to the dish and baste with the sauce. Microwave on HIGH for 2 minutes. Serve at once.

Freezability

Sweet and Sour Pork Balls will freeze well for up to 3 months.

Chinese pork and pasta

Pasta twists or spirals make this stir-fried pork and vegetable concoction a good hearty dish to satisfy after work appetites.

FOR ONE		FOR TWO
20 ml/4 tsp	soy sauce	45 ml/3 tbsp
10 ml/2 tsp	sherry	20 ml/4 tsp
10 ml/2 tsp	cornflour	20 ml/4 tsp
	salt and freshly ground black pepper	
100 g/4 oz	pork fillet, cubed	225 g/8 oz
50 g/2 oz	dried pasta twirls or spirals	100 g/4 oz
300 ml/½ pint	boiling water	450 ml/¾ pint
7.5 ml/1½ tsp	oil	15 ml/1 tbsp
¼	green pepper, cored, seeded and sliced	½
¼	red pepper, cored, seeded and sliced	½
2	spring onions, chopped	4
40 g/1½ oz	beansprouts	75 g/3 oz

For one —

* Mix the soy sauce with the sherry, cornflour and salt and pepper to taste, bending well. Add the pork fillet and leave to marinate for 30 minutes.
* Place the pasta in a deep bowl with the boiling water. Cover and microwave on HIGH for 12-14 minutes then allow to stand for 5-10 minutes until tender. Drain and refresh under cold running water.
* Preheat a browning dish on HIGH for 8 minutes or according to the manufacturer's instructions.
* Add the oil to the browning dish and swirl to coat the base of the dish. Microwave on HIGH for a further 1 minute.
* Remove the pork from the marinade with a slotted spoon and add to the browning dish. Turn quickly in the hot oil to brown evenly on all sides. Add the pepper and microwave on HIGH for 2 minutes, stirring once.
* Add the spring onions and beansprouts, blending well. Microwave on HIGH for 3 minutes, stirring once.
* Stir in the cooked pasta and marinade, blending well. Microwave on HIGH for 1 minute, stirring twice until the sauce is boiling and is thickened. Serve at once.

For two ——

- Mix the soy sauce with the sherry, cornflour and salt and pepper to taste, bending well. Add the pork fillet and leave to marinate for 30 minutes.
- Place the pasta in a deep bowl with the boiling water. Cover and microwave on HIGH for 12-14 minutes then allow to stand for 5-10 minutes until tender. Drain and refresh under cold running water.
- Preheat a browning dish on HIGH for 8 minutes or according to the manufacturer's instructions.
- Add the oil to the browning dish and swirl to coat the base of the dish. Microwave on HIGH for a further 1 minute.
- Remove the pork from the marinade with a slotted spoon and add to the browning dish. Turn quickly in the hot oil to brown evenly on all sides. Add the pepper and microwave on HIGH for 3½ minutes, stirring once.
- Add the spring onions and beansprouts, blending well. Microwave on HIGH for 4½-5 minutes, stirring once.
- Stir in the cooked pasta and marinade, blending well. Microwave on HIGH for 1½-2 minutes, stirring twice until the sauce is boiling and is thickened. Serve at once.

Honey glazed pork chops

This quick and easy recipe brings new life to ordinary mid-week pork chops. The combination of cider and honey makes the meat tender and juicy while adding a delicious flavour.

FOR ONE		FOR TWO
1	large pork loin chop(s)	2
	salt and freshly ground black pepper	
7.5 ml/1½ tsp	clear honey	15 ml/1 tbsp
45 ml/3 tbsp	dry cider	75 ml/5 tbsp
2.5 ml/½ tsp	dried sage	5 ml/1 tsp

For one ——

* Preheat a browning dish on HIGH for 8 minutes or according to the manufacturer's instructions.
* Season the pork with salt and pepper to taste. Add to the browning dish then turn over quickly to brown evenly on both sides. Transfer to a shallow dish.
* Mix the honey with the cider and sage. Pour over the chops and microwave on HIGH for 5-7 minutes, turning over and basting once. Leave to stand, covered, for 3 minutes.
* Serve the pork chop with the sauce poured over.

For two ——

* Preheat a browning dish on HIGH for 8 minutes or according to the manufacturer's instructions.
* Season the pork with salt and pepper to taste. Add to the browning dish then turn over quickly to brown evenly on both sides. Transfer to a shallow dish.
* Mix the honey with the cider and sage. Pour over the chops and microwave on HIGH for 12-14 minutes, turning over and basting once. Leave to stand, covered, for 3 minutes.
* Serve the pork chops with the sauce poured over.

Danish Véronique

Danish Véronique is the ideal dish to consider and cook when entertaining – succulent pink gammon steaks cooked in a creamy sauce with black grapes. Serve with a selection of perfectly cooked vegetables.

FOR ONE		FOR TWO
1 x 175 g/6 oz	gammon steak(s)	2 x 175 g/6 oz
30 ml/2 tbsp	dry white wine	60 ml/4 tbsp
¼	small onion, finely chopped	½
15 g/½ oz	butter	25 g/1 oz
15 g/½ oz	flour	25 g/1 oz
75 ml/5 tbsp	milk	150 ml/¼ pint
15 ml/1 tbsp	single cream	30 ml/2 tbsp
	freshly ground black pepper	
50 g/2 oz	black grapes, halved and seeded	100 g/4 oz
	fresh dill sprigs, to garnish	

For one ——

- Remove the rind from the gammon and snip the fat with kitchen scissors at regular intervals to prevent it curling during cooking. Place in a shallow dish with the wine and onion. Cover and microwave on MEDIUM for 8 minutes until cooked.
- Place the butter in a bowl and microwave on HIGH for ½ minute to melt. Add the flour, blending well. Gradually add the milk and the strained juices from the gammon. Microwave on HIGH for 1-2 minutes, stirring three times until smooth.
- Stir in the cream and pepper to taste. Add half the grapes and microwave on HIGH for ½ minute to reheat.
- To serve, pour the sauce over the gammon, garnish with the remaining grapes and the fresh dill sprigs.

For two ——

- Remove the rind from the gammon and snip the fat with kitchen scissors at regular intervals to prevent it curling during cooking. Place in a dish with the wine and onion. Cover and microwave on MEDIUM for 13-15 minutes until cooked.
- Place the butter in a bowl and microwave on HIGH for ¾ minute to melt. Add the flour, blending well. Gradually add the milk and the strained juices from the gammon. Microwave on HIGH for 3½ minutes, stirring three times until smooth.
- Stir in the cream and pepper to taste. Add half the grapes and microwave on HIGH for 1 minute to reheat.
- To serve, pour the sauce over the gammon, garnish with the remaining grapes and the fresh dill sprigs.

Gingered bacon with pineapple

Pineapple makes a tasty addition to any gammon or back dish – here it is combined with ginger and lemon juice to make a spicy sauce for bacon chops.

FOR ONE		FOR TWO
2 x 75 g/3 oz	bacon chops	4 x 75 g/3 oz
½ x 225 g/8 oz	can pineapple slices in natural juice	1 x 225 g/8 oz
30 ml/2 tbsp	dry white wine or vermouth	60 ml/4 tbsp
7.5 ml/1½ tsp	lemon juice	15 ml/1 tbsp
7.5 ml/1½ tsp	dark brown sugar	15 ml/1 tbsp
5 ml/1 tsp	ground ginger	10 ml/2 tsp
5 ml/1 tsp	Worcestershire sauce	10 ml/2 tsp
	dash of Tabasco sauce	
1.25 ml/¼ tsp	Dijon mustard	2.5 ml/½ tsp
5 ml/1 tsp	cornflour	10 ml/2 tsp
	watercress sprigs, to garnish	

For one ——

- Using kitchen scissors, snip the bacon fat at regular intervals to prevent it from curling during cooking. Place in a shallow dish.
- Drain the juice from the pineapple and mix with the wine or vermouth, lemon juice, sugar, ginger, Worcestershire sauce, Tabasco, mustard and cornflour, blending well.
- Pour over the chops, cover and microwave on HIGH for 3½-4 minutes until tender, turning over once.
- Arrange the pineapple slices on top of the chop, cover and microwave on HIGH for ¾ minute. Leave to stand, covered for 5 minutes. Garnish with watercress sprigs and serve at once.

For two ——

- Using kitchen scissors, snip the bacon fat at regular intervals to prevent it from curling during cooking. Place in a shallow dish.
- Drain the juice from the pineapple and mix with the wine or vermouth, lemon juice, sugar, ginger, Worcestershire sauce, Tabasco, mustard and cornflour, blending well.
- Pour over the chops, cover and microwave on HIGH for 5 minutes until tender, turning over once.
- Arrange the pineapple slices on top of the chop, cover and microwave on HIGH for 1 minute. Leave to stand, covered for 5 minutes. Garnish with watercress sprigs and serve at once.

Cook's tip

For a strong flavour, and if time permits, marinate the bacon chops in the sauce for up to 8 hours before cooking.

Quick step chilli with rice

Chilli, ready for eating in 12 minutes? Seriously? You better believe it because this high-speed version short-cuts this 'once-upon-a-time' slow cooked favourite but doesn't sacrifice on flavour one little bit. It even comes with the rice included for a complete meal. A real winner dinner …

FOR ONE		FOR TWO
65 g/2½ oz	minced beef	150 g/5 oz
25 g/1 oz	onion, chopped	50 g/2 oz
1	garlic clove(s), peeled and crushed	2
15 ml/1 tbsp	tomato paste	30 ml/2 tbsp
5 ml/1 tsp	hot or mild chilli powder (to taste)	10 ml/2 tsp
5 ml/1 tsp	ground cumin	10 ml/2 tsp
5 ml/1 tsp	smoked paprika	10 ml/2 tsp
5 ml/1 tsp	dried oregano	10 ml/2 tsp
40 g/1½ oz	basmati rice	75 g/3 oz
200 ml/7 fl oz	beef stock	400 ml/14 fl oz
15 ml/1 tbsp	olive oil	30 ml/2 tbsp
100 g/4 oz	cooked or canned kidney beans (or canned kidney beans in chilli sauce)	225 g/8 oz
15 ml/1 tbsp	instant beef gravy granules	30 ml/2 tbsp
	salt and freshly ground black pepper	
	plain yogurt and coriander leaves to garnish (optional)	

For one ——

- Place the beef, onion, garlic, tomato paste, chilli powder, cumin, paprika, oregano, rice, half of the stock and the oil in a dish and mix thoroughly. Cover and microwave on HIGH for 5 minutes.
- Remove from the microwave, stir well and add the remaining beef stock and kidney beans. Mix again, re-cover and microwave on HIGH for 2½ minutes.
- Remove from the microwave, stir well then mix in the gravy granules with seasoning to taste. Re-cover and microwave on HIGH for a further 1½ minutes. Leave to stand for 3 minutes, before serving garnished with a little plain yogurt and coriander leaves if liked.

For two

- Place the beef, onion, garlic, tomato paste, chilli powder, cumin, paprika, oregano, rice, half of the stock and the oil in a dish and mix thoroughly. Cover and microwave on HIGH for 8 minutes.
- Remove from the microwave, stir well and add the remaining beef stock and kidney beans. Mix again, re-cover and microwave on HIGH for 3½-4 minutes.
- Remove from the microwave, stir well then mix in the gravy granules with seasoning to taste. Re-cover and microwave on HIGH for a further 2-2½ minutes. Leave to stand for 3 minutes, before serving garnished with a little plain yogurt and coriander leaves if liked.

Beef Stroganoff

It is essential to follow the timings in this recipe exactly for mouth-wateringly tender strips of beef. Serve with boiled rice and a green salad to make a quick and delicious meal.

FOR ONE		FOR TWO
7 g/¼ oz	butter	15 g/½ oz
175 g/6 oz	beef fillet, cut into thin strips	350 g/12 oz
½	small onion, peeled and chopped	1
50 g/2 oz	button mushrooms, wiped and finely sliced	100 g/4 oz
7 g/¼ oz	plain flour	15 g/½ oz
25 ml/1 fl oz	dry white wine	50 ml/2 fl oz
	salt and freshly ground black pepper	
45 ml/ 3 tbsp	soured cream	75 ml/5 tbsp
	chopped fresh parsley, to garnish	

For one

- Preheat a browning dish on HIGH for 8 minutes or according to the manufacturer's instructions. Add the butter and microwave on HIGH for ½ minute to melt.
- Add the beef and turn quickly in the hot butter to brown evenly on all sides. Microwave on HIGH for 1-2 minutes until tender and pink.
- Remove the meat from the dish with a slotted spoon and set aside. Add the onion and mushrooms to the juice in the dish and microwave on HIGH for 2 minutes, stirring once.

- ◆ Stir in the flour, blending well. Gradually add the wine, then the beef and salt and pepper to taste. Microwave on HIGH for ¾-1 minute, stirring twice. Stir in the soured cream, blending well. Serve at once garnished with the chopped parsley.

For two

- ◆ Preheat a browning dish on HIGH for 8 minutes or according to the manufacturer's instructions. Add the butter and microwave on HIGH for ½ minute to melt.
- ◆ Add the beef and turn quickly in the hot butter to brown evenly on all sides. Microwave on HIGH for 2-3 minutes until tender and pink.
- ◆ Remove the meat from the dish with a slotted spoon and set aside. Add the onion and mushrooms to the juice in the dish and microwave on HIGH for 3-3½ minutes, stirring once.
- ◆ Stir in the flour, blending well. Gradually add the wine, then the beef and salt and pepper to taste. Microwave on HIGH for 1½-2 minutes, stirring twice. Stir in the soured cream, blending well. Serve at once garnished with the chopped parsley.

Simplest spaghetti Bolognese

Perfectly cooked spaghetti and a delicious version of the famous Italian Bolognese sauce feature in this easy main meal. Serve with freshly grated Parmesan cheese for sprinkling and a crisp side salad.

FOR ONE		FOR TWO
50 g/2 oz	dried spaghetti	100 g/4 oz
500 ml/14 fl oz	boiling water	1 litre/1¾ pints
	salt and freshly ground black pepper	
	BOLOGNESE SAUCE	
100 g/4 oz	minced beef	225 g/8 oz
½	small onion, peeled and finely chopped	1
2.5 ml/½ tsp	garlic purée	5 ml/1 tsp
½	small green pepper, cored, seeded and chopped	1
7.5 ml/1½ tsp	tomato purée	15 ml/1 tbsp
½ x 225 g/8 oz	can chopped tomatoes	1 x 225 g/8 oz
2.5 ml/½ tsp	Worcestershire sauce	3 ml/¾ tsp
2.5 ml/½ tsp	dried oregano	5 ml/1 tsp

For one ——

- Break the spaghetti in half and place in a deep bowl with the water and salt to taste. Cover and microwave on HIGH for 10 minutes, stirring once. Leave to stand, covered, for 5 minutes until tender.
- Place the beef, onion, garlic purée and pepper in a bowl. Microwave on HIGH for 2 minutes, stirring once.
- Add the tomato purée, tomatoes, Worcestershire sauce, oregano and salt and pepper to taste, blending well. Cover and microwave on HIGH for 5 minutes, stirring twice. Leave to stand for 2-3 minutes.
- Drain the spaghetti and place on a serving plate. Spoon over the Bolognese sauce and serve at once.

For two ——

- Break the spaghetti in half and place in a deep bowl with the water and salt to taste. Cover and microwave on HIGH for 10 minutes, stirring once. Leave to stand, covered, for 5 minutes until tender.
- Place the beef, onion, garlic purée and pepper in a bowl. Microwave on HIGH for 3½-4 minutes, stirring once.
- Add the tomato purée, tomatoes, Worcestershire sauce, oregano and salt and pepper to taste, blending well. Cover and microwave on HIGH for 10 minutes, stirring twice. Leave to stand for 2-3 minutes.
- Drain the spaghetti and place on a serving plate. Spoon over the Bolognese sauce and serve at once.

Stuffed baked onions

Large, Spanish onions are very good for 'hollowing out' and stuffing with a savoury mixture.

FOR ONE		FOR TWO
1	large Spanish onion(s), peeled	2
5 ml/1 tsp	oil	10 ml/2 tsp
100 g/4 oz	minced beef	225 g/8 oz
7.5 ml/1½ tsp	tomato purée	15 ml/1 tbsp
25 g/1 oz	clean mushrooms (see method)	50 g/2 oz
5 ml/1 tsp	flour	10 ml/2 tsp
	pinch of dried mixed herbs	
	salt and freshly ground black pepper	
	parsley sprigs to garnish	

For one —

- Slice the top of the mushrooms, remove the root end and discard. Place in a shallow dish and cover. Microwave on HIGH for 4-6 minutes until almost tender.
- Scoop out the centre of the onion with a serrated teaspoon or a sharp knife and chop finely.
- Place the oil, chopped onion and beef in a bowl. Microwave on HIGH for 3 minutes, stirring once.
- Add the tomato purée, mushrooms, flour, herbs and salt and pepper to taste, blending well. Microwave on HIGH for 2 minutes, stirring once.
- Spoon the beef mixture into the onion case, piling it high. Return to the dish, cover and microwave on HIGH for 2-3 minutes until the onion is tender. Serve hot, garnished with parsley sprigs.

For two —

- Slice the top of the mushrooms, remove the root end and discard. Place in a suitable dish and cover. Microwave on HIGH for 9-11 minutes until almost tender.
- Scoop out the centre of the onion with a serrated teaspoon or a sharp knife and chop finely.
- Place the oil, chopped onion and beef in a bowl. Microwave on HIGH for 5-6 minutes, stirring once.
- Add the tomato purée, mushrooms, flour, herbs and salt and pepper to taste, blending well. Microwave on HIGH for 3-4 minutes, stirring once.
- Spoon the beef mixture into the onion case, piling it high. Return to the dish, cover and microwave on HIGH for 4-6 minutes until the onion is tender. Serve hot, garnished with parsley sprigs.

Chilli minced beef and beans

Condensed oxtail soup makes a delicious thick savoury base for this Mexican inspired dish.

FOR ONE		FOR TWO
100 g/4 oz	minced beef	225 g/8 oz
½	small onion, peeled and chopped	1
5 ml/1 tsp	chilli powder	10 ml/2 tsp
½ x 225 g/8 oz	can chopped tomatoes	1 x 225 g/8 oz
¼ x 298 g/10 oz	can condensed oxtail soup	½ x 298 g/10 oz
50 g/2 oz	cooked red kidney or butter beans	100 g/4 oz
1	small celery stick(s), scrubbed and chopped	2

For one —

- Place the beef and onion in a bowl. Cover and microwave on HIGH for 2 minutes. Break up with a fork and stir in the chilli powder, blending well.
- Add the tomatoes and soup, blending well. Cover and microwave on HIGH for 5 minutes, stirring once.
- Add the beans and celery, blending well. Cover and microwave on HIGH for 2 minutes, stirring once. Allow to stand for 3 minutes before serving with rice or corn chips.

For two —

- Place the beef and onion in a bowl. Cover and microwave on HIGH for 3½-4 minutes. Break up with a fork and stir in the chilli powder, blending well.
- Add the tomatoes and soup, blending well. Cover and microwave on HIGH for 10 minutes, stirring once.
- Add the beans and celery, blending well. Cover and microwave on HIGH for 3-4 minutes, stirring once. Allow to stand for 3 minutes before serving with rice or corn chips.

Sausage pilau

Sausages are endlessly versatile, main meal ingredients and when combined with onion, rice, sweetcorn, beans and mushrooms make a worthy and hearty main course.

FOR ONE		FOR TWO
2	pork sausages	4
5 ml/1 tsp	oil	10 ml/2 tsp
½	small onion, peeled and chopped	1
25 g/1 oz	long-grain rice	50 g/2 oz
25 g/1 oz	sweetcorn kernels	50 g/2 oz
25 g/1 oz	green beans	50 g/2 oz
25 g/1 oz	sliced mushrooms	50 g/2 oz
5 ml/1 tsp	Worcestershire sauce	10 ml/2 tsp
	salt and freshly ground black pepper	
150 ml/¼ pint	chicken stock	300 ml/½ pint

For one

- Prick the sausages and place on a plate. Cover with absorbent kitchen towel and microwave on HIGH for 1½-2 minutes, turning over once. Cut into bite-sized pieces and set aside.
- Place the oil and onion in a bowl. Cover and microwave on HIGH for 1 minute. Add the rice, cover and microwave on HIGH for 1 minute.
- Add the sweetcorn, beans, mushrooms, Worcestershire sauce, salt and pepper to taste and stock, blending well. Cover and microwave on HIGH for 3 minutes. Reduce the power setting and microwave on MEDIUM for 12 minutes, stirring once. Add the sausages, blending well. Leave to stand, covered, for 5 minutes. Serve with a salad.

For two

- Prick the sausages and place on a plate. Cover with absorbent kitchen towel and microwave on HIGH for 3-3½ minutes, turning over once. Cut into bite-sized pieces and set aside.
- Place the oil and onion in a bowl. Cover and microwave on HIGH for 1½ minutes. Add the rice, cover and microwave on HIGH for 1½ minutes.
- Add the sweetcorn, beans, mushrooms, Worcestershire sauce, salt and pepper to taste and stock, blending well. Cover and microwave on HIGH for 3 minutes. Reduce the power setting and microwave on MEDIUM for 12 minutes, stirring once. Add the sausages, blending well. Leave to stand, covered, for 5 minutes. Serve with a salad.

Chorizo Jambalaya

This easy to prep Jambalaya is a cinch to make with easy-cook rice and a little chorizo, frozen corn kernels and a dash of Cajun seasoning – but do check the heat or spiciness of your chorizo before judiciously adding the latter – some can be quite hot, hot, hot! You can of course substitute the chorizo with any other spicy cooked sausage.

FOR ONE		FOR TWO
100 g/4 oz	canned chopped tomatoes	225 g/8 oz
½	garlic clove, chopped	1
50 g/2 oz	chopped onion	100 g/ 4 oz
125 g/4½ oz	easy-cook rice	250 g/9 oz
200 ml/7 fl oz	hot water	400 ml/14 fl oz
¼	red pepper, chopped	½
50 g/2 oz	chorizo, coarsely chopped	100 g/4 oz
50 g/2 oz	frozen sweetcorn kernels	100 g/4 oz
2.5-2.75 ml/½-¾ tsp	Cajun seasoning	5-7.5 ml/1-1½ tsp
	salt and freshly ground black pepper	

For one ——

* Place the tomatoes in a dish with the garlic, onion and rice. Stir in the water, red pepper, chorizo, sweetcorn, Cajun seasoning and salt and pepper to taste, mixing well.
* Cover and microwave on HIGH for 10 minutes.
* Remove from the microwave, stir well, and microwave, uncovered, on MEDIUM for a further 8 minutes or until the rice is just cooked. Cover and leave to stand for 5 minutes before stirring with a fork to loosen the rice grains to serve.

For two ——

* Place the tomatoes in a dish with the garlic, onion and rice. Stir in the water, red pepper, chorizo, sweetcorn, Cajun seasoning and salt and pepper to taste, mixing well.
* Cover and microwave on HIGH for 14 minutes.
* Remove from the microwave, stir well, and microwave, uncovered, on MEDIUM for a further 10-12 minutes or until the rice is just cooked. Cover and leave to stand for 5 minutes before stirring with a fork to loosen the rice grains to serve.

Poultry

Stuffed pancetta chicken breasts

I haven't quite given up on cooking a whole family-sized chicken but often resort to this recipe when I fancy roast chicken without all the time-costly fanfare involved with a large bird. It looks and tastes impressive especially if sliced to reveal the stuffing before serving on its bed of flavoursome chickpeas.

FOR ONE		FOR TWO
1 x 125 g/4 oz	skinless chicken breast(s)	2 x 125 g/4 oz
30 ml/2 tbsp	herby cream cheese	60 ml/4 tbsp
3	black olives, sliced	6
30 g/1¼ oz	pancetta rashers	60 g/2½ oz
50 g/2 oz	cooked chickpeas	100 g/4 oz
75 ml/5 tbsp	canned chopped tomatoes	150 ml/¼ pint
15 ml/1 tbsp	extra virgin oil	30 ml/2 tbsp
5 ml/1 tsp	chives, snipped	10 ml/2 tsp
	salt and freshly ground black pepper	

For one ——

* Prepare the chicken breast for stuffing by cutting along one side to open up like a pocket, but take care not to totally cut through.
* Mix the cream cheese with two-thirds of the olives and use to stuff the chicken breast, fold over to enclose the filling. Wrap the pancetta around the breast and secure if liked with a wooden skewer or keep the pancetta in position by tucking underneath to secure the joins.
* Mix the chickpeas with the tomatoes, oil, chives, seasoning to taste and remaining olives in a dish and position the chicken breast on top. Microwave, uncovered, on HIGH for 6-7 minutes (depending upon its size and thickness). Leave to stand for 2 minutes before slicing to serve on the bed of chickpeas.

For two ——

* Prepare the chicken breasts for stuffing by cutting along one side of each to open up like a pocket, but take care not to totally cut through.

- Mix the cream cheese with two-thirds of the olives and use to stuff the chicken breasts, fold over to enclose the filling. Wrap the pancetta around the breasts and secure if liked with wooden skewers or keep the pancetta in position by tucking underneath to secure the joins.
- Mix the chickpeas with the tomatoes, oil, chives, seasoning to taste and remaining olives in a dish and position the chicken breasts on top. Microwave, uncovered, on HIGH for 10-12 minutes (depending upon their size and thickness). Leave to stand for 2 minutes before slicing to serve on the bed of chickpeas.

Chicken with mushroom cream sauce

Canned soup makes a flavoursome base for a casserole or a sauce and has the added advantage that it doesn't need thickening. Here celery soup adds flavour to chicken joints.

FOR ONE		FOR TWO
7 g/¼ oz	butter	15 g/½ oz
1	chicken joint(s), skinned	2
10 ml/2 tsp	dry sherry	20 ml/4 tsp
75 ml/5 tbsp	cream of celery soup	150 ml/¼ pint
25 g/1 oz	mushrooms, sliced	50 g/2 oz
45 ml/3 tbsp	single cream	75 ml/5 tbsp
	salt and freshly ground black pepper	

For one ——

- Place the butter in a dish and microwave on HIGH for ½ minute to melt. Add the chicken and microwave on HIGH for 1½-2 minutes, turning over once.
- Add the sherry and soup, blending well. Cover and microwave on HIGH for 7 minutes. Add the mushrooms and microwave for 1 minute.
- Stir in the cream and salt and pepper to taste, blending well. Cover and allow to stand for 3 minutes before serving.

For two

- Place the butter in a dish and microwave on HIGH for ¾ minute to melt. Add the chicken and microwave on HIGH for 3-4 minutes, turning over once.
- Add the sherry and soup, blending well. Cover and microwave on HIGH for 14 minutes. Add the mushrooms and microwave for 2 minutes.
- Stir in the cream and salt and pepper to taste, blending well. Cover and allow to stand for 3 minutes before serving.

Chicken bean bake

A nourishing gratin style dish, Chicken Bean Bake can be made using leftover chicken or turkey or a bought ready-cooked portion of the same. Serve with a crispy salad.

FOR ONE		FOR TWO
150 ml/¼ pint	hot White Sauce (see page 149)	300 ml/½ pint
75 g/3 oz	cooked chicken, chopped	175 g/6 oz
100 g/4 oz	cammed baked beans in tomato sauce	225 g/8 oz
25 g/1 oz	pasta twists, cooked	50 g/2 oz
25 g/1 oz	Cheddar cheese, grated	50 g/2 oz
	salt and freshly ground black pepper	
1 small	tomato, sliced	1 large
7 g/¼ oz	flaked almonds	15 g/½ oz

For one

- Mix the white sauce with the chicken, blending well.
- Add the beans, cooked pasta and three-quarters of the cheese, blending well. Season to taste with salt and pepper and place in a shallow heatproof dish.
- Arrange the tomato slices on top, sprinkle with the remaining cheese and scatter over the almonds. Microwave on HIGH for 2-3 minutes. Brown under a preheated grill if liked. Serve hot.

For two

- Mix the white sauce with the chicken, blending well.
- Add the beans, cooked pasta and three-quarters of the cheese, blending well. Season to taste with salt and pepper and place in a shallow heatproof dish.

- Arrange the tomato slices on top, sprinkle with the remaining cheese and scatter over the almonds. Microwave on HIGH for 4-5 minutes. Brown under a preheated grill if liked. Serve hot.

Cook's tip

This dish is a good combination of leftovers and storecupboard standbys.

Stuffed roast poussins

Tender, sweet and succulent baby chickens, stuffed with a couscous, dried fruit and nut stuffing, make delicious eating when roasted and basted with a herby butter.

FOR ONE		FOR TWO
60 ml/4 tbsp	cooked couscous	120 ml/8 tbsp
30 ml/2 tbsp	mixed chopped dried fruit (such as dried apricots, soured cherries, cranberries and raisins)	60 ml/4 tbsp
10 ml/2 tsp	flaked almonds	20 ml/4 tsp
5 ml/1 tsp	chopped fresh parsley	10 ml/2 tsp
	salt and freshly ground black pepper	
1	poussin(s), cleaned	2
25 g/1 oz	butter, softened	40 g/1½ oz
15 ml/1 tbsp	chopped fresh mixed herbs	30 ml/2 tbsp
	watercress sprigs, to garnish	

For one ——

- Make the stuffing by mixing the couscous with the dried fruit, almonds, parsley and salt and pepper to taste. Add about one-third of the softened butter and mix well. Stuff the poussin with the prepared mixture and truss with string to make a neat shape.
- Preheat a browning dish on HIGH for 8 minutes or according to the manufacturer's instructions.
- Add another one-third of the butter and swirl to coat the base of the dish. Add the poussin, breast-side down, and turn quickly to brown the breast on each side. Remove from the dish, dot the breast with the remaining butter and sprinkle with the herbs. Place in a small roasting bag on an upturned saucer in a dish.
- Reduce the power setting and microwave on MEDIUM for 9-11 minutes. Leave to stand, covered for 10 minutes. Serve hot garnished with watercress.

For two

* Make the stuffing by mixing the couscous with the dried fruit, almonds, parsley and salt and pepper to taste. Add about one-third of the softened butter and mix well. Stuff the poussins with the prepared mixture and truss with string to make a neat shape.
* Preheat a browning dish on HIGH for 8 minutes or according to the manufacturer's instructions.
* Add another one-third of the butter and swirl to coat the base of the dish. Add the poussins, breast-side down, and turn quickly to brown the breasts on each side. Remove from the dish, dot each breast with the remaining butter and sprinkle with the herbs. Place in a medium roasting bag on an upturned saucer in a dish.
* Reduce the power setting and microwave on MEDIUM for 18-20 minutes. Leave to stand, covered for 10 minutes. Serve hot garnished with watercress.

Spiced chicken and mango

This Eastern spiced dish relies upon the cunning combination of a few spices with chicken, tomatoes and mango. Serve with Creamed Coconut and Pine Nut Rice (see page 145).

FOR ONE		FOR TWO
2.5 ml/½ tsp	oil	5 ml/1 tsp
½	large onion, peeled and sliced	1
¼	red pepper, cored, seeded and sliced	½
¼	green pepper, cored, seeded and sliced	½
pinch	ground ginger	1.25 ml/¼ tsp
5 ml/1 tsp	ground coriander	7.5 ml/1½ tsp
7.5 ml/1½ tsp	garam masala	15 ml/1 tbsp
2.5 ml/½ tsp	ground cumin	5 ml/1 tsp
2.5 ml/½ tsp	finely grated lemon rind	5 ml/1 tsp
1 x 225 g/8 oz	can chopped tomatoes	1 x 397 g/14 oz
	salt and freshly ground black pepper	
150 g/5 oz	cooked chicken, skinned and cut into bite-sized pieces	275 g/10 oz
½	ripe mango, peeled, stoned and cubed	1
45 ml/3 tbsp	set natural yogurt	75 ml/5 tbsp
2.5 ml/½ tsp	mint sauce	5 ml/1 tsp
	chopped fresh coriander, to garnish	

For one ——

- Place the oil, onion, peppers, ginger, ground coriander, garam masala and cumin in a bowl. Cover and microwave on HIGH for 2 minutes, stirring once.
- Add the lemon rind, tomatoes and salt and pepper to taste, blending well. Cover and microwave on HIGH for 2 minutes, stirring once.
- Add the chicken and fresh mango, blending well. Cover, reduce the power setting and microwave on MEDIUM for 5 minutes, stirring twice.
- Meanwhile blend the yogurt with the mint sauce.
- Serve hot drizzled with minted yogurt and garnished with chopped coriander.

For two ——

- Place the oil, onion, peppers, ginger, ground coriander, garam masala and cumin in a bowl. Cover and microwave on HIGH for 4 minutes, stirring once.
- Add the lemon rind, tomatoes and salt and pepper to taste, blending well. Cover and microwave on HIGH for 2-3 minutes, stirring once.
- Add the chicken and fresh mango, blending well. Cover, reduce the power setting and microwave on MEDIUM for 10 minutes, stirring twice.
- Meanwhile blend the yogurt with the mint sauce.
- Serve hot drizzled with minted yogurt and garnished with chopped coriander.

Cook's tip

Peeling a mango can be quite an awesome task – here is the simplest and most rewarding way. Spear one end of the mango with a fork. Using the fork to hold the mango, cut the fruit's skin lengthways with a sharp knife to divide into 4 sections. Grip each section of skin between your thumb and the knife and gently pull away to strip off the skin.

Easy peasy chicken enchiladas

If you have never thought of making enchiladas in the microwave before then you are in for a new tasty treat in double quick time. Made this way, chicken enchiladas emerge hassle and stress free for a speedy mid-week meal especially if you have storecupboard enchilada sauce, taco seasoning mix and some rotisserie chicken to hand. You can use whole wheat or corn tortillas for this recipe and it is worth seeking out some Mexican blend cheese for authenticity.

FOR ONE		FOR TWO
75 g/3 oz	shredded rotisserie cooked chicken	175 g/6 oz
125 g/4 oz	mild enchilada sauce	250 g/8 oz
1.25 ml/¼ tsp	taco seasoning mix	2.5 ml/½ tsp
2 x 27 g/1 oz	slices Mexican cheese, grated or cut into strips	4 x 27 g/1 oz
30 ml/2 tbsp	chopped fresh coriander	60 ml/4 tbsp
1	large whole wheat or corn tortilla(s)	2

For one ——

- Mix the chicken with half of the enchilada sauce, the seasoning mix, half of the cheese and half of the coriander in a bowl.
- Fill the tortilla with this mixture and roll to seal. Place, seam side down, in a dish and cover with the remaining enchilada sauce and cheese.
- Cover very loosely with some kitchen paper to prevent spattering (but do not allow the paper to touch the enchilada or it may stick). Microwave, on HIGH for 3 minutes.
- Allow to stand for 1 minute before serving sprinkled with the remaining coriander.

For two ——

- Mix the chicken with half of the enchilada sauce, the seasoning mix, half of the cheese and half of the coriander in a bowl.
- Fill the tortillas with this mixture and roll to seal. Place, seam side down, in a dish and cover with the remaining enchilada sauce and cheese.

- Cover very loosely with some kitchen paper to prevent spattering (but do not allow the paper to touch the enchilada or it may stick). Microwave, on HIGH for 4-5 minutes.
- Allow to stand for 1 minute before serving sprinkled with the remaining coriander.

Turkey breast parcels

This is the microwave answer to cooking meat in a foil parcel or 'papillote', where the foil is replaced by a plastic roast or cook bag. Use chicken fillets or breasts if turkey breast escalopes are unavailable.

FOR ONE		FOR TWO
1 x 225 g/8 oz	turkey breast escalope(s)	2 x 225 g/8 oz
7 g/¼ oz	butter	15 g/½ oz
1	tomato(es), skinned and coarsely chopped	2
1	celery stick(s), scrubbed and finely sliced	2
25 g/1 oz	sweetcorn kernels	50 g/2 oz
25 g/1 oz	cooked ham, chopped	50 g/2 oz
	salt and freshly ground black pepper	
30 ml/2 tbsp	chicken stock	60 ml/4 tbsp
	chopped fresh parsley, to garnish	

For one ———

- Rub the turkey with the butter and place in a small roast or cook bag.
- Mix the tomatoes with the celery, sweetcorn, ham and salt and pepper to taste, blending well. Spoon on top of the turkey. Add the stock to the bag, seal loosely with an elastic band, plastic tie or string.
- Microwave on HIGH for 2 minutes. Reduce the power setting to MEDIUM and cook for a further 5-7 minutes until tender.
- Transfer to a serving plate, but open the bag (taking care as the steam released can burn) and lift out the turkey and vegetable mixture.
- Garnish with chopped parsley and serve hot.

For two

- Rub the turkey with the butter and place in a roast or cook bag.
- Mix the tomatoes with the celery, sweetcorn, ham and salt and pepper to taste, blending well. Spoon on top of the turkey. Add the stock to the bag, seal loosely with an elastic band, plastic tie or string.
- Microwave on HIGH for 3½ minutes. Reduce the power setting to MEDIUM and cook for a further 8-10 minutes until tender.
- Transfer to a serving plate, but open the bag (taking care as the steam released can burn) and lift out the turkey and vegetable mixture.
- Garnish with chopped parsley and serve hot.

Chinese duck

Duck breasts are often available in supermarkets ready trimmed and prepared and are deliciously easy and quick to cook in the microwave.

FOR ONE		FOR TWO
1 x 175 g/6 oz	duck breast(s)	2 x 175 g/6 oz
MARINADE AND BASTE		
7.5 ml/1½ tsp	soy sauce	15 ml/1 tbsp
20 ml/4 tsp	clear honey	40 ml/8 tsp
20 ml/4 tsp	sesame oil	40 ml/8 tsp
30 ml/2 tbsp	dry sherry or orange juice	60 ml/4 tbsp
2.5 ml/½ tsp	finely chopped fresh root ginger	5 ml/1 tsp
2.5 ml/½ tsp	finely grated orange rind	5 ml/1 tsp
½	small onion, peeled and chopped	1
	pinch of Chinese 5 spice powder	
	freshly ground black pepper	
	spring onion curls, to garnish	

For one

- Using a sharp knife, make diagonal cuts across the skin of the duck to make a diamond or chequered cut pattern.
- Mix the soy sauce with the honey, oil, sherry or orange juice, ginger, orange rind, onion, Chinese 5 spice powder and black pepper to taste, blending well. Spoon over the duck and leave to marinate for 2-4 hours, turning occasionally.

- Remove the duck from the marinade with a slotted spoon and place on a roasting rack. Brush with a little of the marinade and microwave on MEDIUM for 6-8 minutes, brushing with the marinade twice and turning over once during cooking. Allow to stand for 3-5 minutes.
- If a crisp skin is preferred quickly brown the duck to crisp under a preheated grill before serving. Carve into thick slices and arrange on a warmed serving plate.
- Garnish with spring onion curls and serve at once with a green vegetable.

For two

- Using a sharp knife, make diagonal cuts across the skin of the duck to make a diamond or chequered cut pattern.
- Mix the soy sauce with the honey, oil, sherry or orange juice, ginger, orange rind, onion, Chinese 5 spice powder and black pepper to taste, blending well. Spoon over the duck and leave to marinate for 2-4 hours, turning occasionally.
- Remove the duck from the marinade with a slotted spoon and place on a roasting rack. Brush with a little of the marinade and microwave on MEDIUM for 12-16 minutes, brushing with the marinade twice and turning over once during cooking. Allow to stand for 3-5 minutes.
- If a crisp skin is preferred quickly brown the duck to crisp under a preheated grill before serving. Carve into thick slices and arrange on a warmed serving plate.
- Garnish with spring onion curls and serve at once with a green vegetable.

Cook's tip

If duck breasts are unavailable use chicken or turkey breasts instead.

Vegan and vegetarian

Vegan lentil ratatouille

This recipe for ratatouille is a variation on the traditional one on page 129 because it mixes all the typical ingredients like peppers, aubergine, courgettes, onions and tomatoes with puy lentils to make it more of a filling main meal not just a side dish. It's just as good – albeit a bit heartier and more nourishing.

FOR ONE		FOR TWO
30 ml/2 tbsp	extra virgin olive oil	60 ml/4 tbsp
40 g/1½ oz	aubergine, chopped	75 g/3 oz
40 g/1½ oz	courgettes, chopped	75 g/3 oz
40 g/1½ oz	red pepper, chopped	75 g/3 oz
30 ml/2 tbsp	red onion, sliced	60 ml/4 tbsp
1	garlic clove(s), crushed	2
75 ml/5 tbsp	canned chopped tomatoes	150 ml/¼ pint
1.25 ml/¼ tsp	turmeric	2.5 ml/½ tsp
60 ml/4 tbsp	cooked puy lentils	120 ml/8 tbsp
2.5 ml/½ tsp	balsamic vinegar	5 ml/1 tsp
	salt and freshly ground black pepper	
7.5 ml/1½ tsp	fresh parsley, chopped	15 ml/1 tbsp
7.5 ml/1½ tsp	fresh coriander, chopped	15 ml/1 tbsp
	lemon juice, to taste	

For one ——

* Place the oil, aubergine, courgettes, red pepper, onion and garlic in a dish. Mix well then microwave, uncovered, on HIGH for 3½ minutes.
* Add the chopped tomatoes, turmeric, lentils, balsamic vinegar and seasoning to taste, mixing well. Microwave, uncovered, on HIGH for 2½ minutes.
* Leave to stand for 1 minute then stir through the parsley, coriander and a squeeze of lemon juice (to taste) to serve.

For two ——

* Place the oil, aubergine, courgettes, red pepper, onion and garlic in a dish. Mix well then microwave, uncovered, on HIGH for 5-5½ minutes.
* Add the chopped tomatoes, turmeric, lentils, balsamic vinegar and seasoning to taste, mixing well. Microwave, uncovered, on HIGH for 4-4½ minutes.

- Leave to stand for 1 minute then stir through the parsley, coriander and a squeeze of lemon juice (to taste) to serve.

Vegetable and taco bean ragout

There's a vast array of pre-prepared beans in sauces that lend themselves beautifully to this simple ragout dish. Here taco beans have been used but you could just as easily replace with cassoulet beans, chilli beans, curried beans or Spanish beans for a tasty and satisfying vegetarian main meal.

FOR ONE		FOR TWO
30 ml/2 tbsp	onion, chopped	60 ml/4 tbsp
1	medium carrot(s), peeled and thinly sliced	2
½	medium potato, cubed	1
1	small leek(s), sliced	2
100 g/4 oz	canned beans in taco sauce	225 g/8 oz
100 g/4 oz	canned chopped tomatoes	225 g/8 oz
7.5 ml/1½ tsp	vegetable gravy granules	15 ml/1 tbsp
15 ml/1 tbsp	fresh parsley, chopped	30 ml/2 tbsp

For one ——

- Place the onion, carrot, potato, leek and 3 tbsp water in a bowl, mixing well. Cover and microwave on HIGH for 4-5 minutes, stirring once halfway through the cooking time. Drain well.
- Add the canned beans in taco sauce, tomatoes and gravy granules, mixing well. Cover and microwave on HIGH for 2 minutes, stirring once.
- Add the parsley and mix well. Serve hot with rice, crusty bread or couscous.

For two ——

- Place the onion, carrot, potato, leek and 5 tbsp water in a bowl, mixing well. Cover and microwave on HIGH for 7-8 minutes, stirring once halfway through the cooking time. Drain well.
- Add the canned beans in taco sauce, tomatoes and gravy granules, mixing well. Cover and microwave on HIGH for 3-3½ minutes, stirring once.
- Add the parsley and mix well. Serve hot with rice, crusty bread or couscous.

Quick bean cassoulet

Look out for canned cassoulet beans in sauce when making this dish, if unavailable use baked beans in tomato sauce.

FOR ONE		FOR TWO
15 g/½ oz	butter	25 g/1 oz
50 g/2 oz	mushrooms sliced	100 g/4 oz
2	tomatoes, skinned, seeded and chopped	4
100 g/4 oz	canned cassoulet beans	225 g/8 oz
	salt and freshly ground black pepper	
	pinch of mixed dried herbs	
25 g/1 oz	wholemeal breadcrumbs or Crispy Croutons (see page 148)	50 g/2 oz

For one

* Place the butter and mushrooms in a serving dish. Microwave on HIGH for 1 minute, stirring once.
* Add the tomatoes, cassoulet beans, salt and pepper to taste and herbs, blending well. Cover and microwave on HIGH for 3 minutes, stirring once.
* Sprinkle with the breadcrumbs or croutons. Brown under a preheated grill, if liked. Serve at once with crusty bread or a salad.

For two

* Place the butter and mushrooms in a serving dish. Microwave on HIGH for 1½ minutes, stirring once.
* Add the tomatoes, cassoulet beans, salt and pepper to taste and herbs, blending well. Cover and microwave on HIGH for 6 minutes, stirring once.
* Sprinkle with the breadcrumbs or croutons. Brown under a preheated grill, if liked. Serve at once with crusty bread or a salad.

Cook's tip

The microwave will speedily help with peeling tomatoes for cooked dishes. Pierce the skin and place on a plate. Microwave on HIGH for 1-2 minutes, depending on number, then peel or strip the skin away easily.

Spaghetti with Napolitan sauce

Fresh wholewheat spaghetti is now available in many supermarkets and combined with this fresh tomato herb sauce makes a hearty, economical and wholesome meat-free main course.

FOR ONE		FOR TWO
100 g/4 oz	fresh wholewheat spaghetti	225 g/8 oz
600 ml/1 pint	herb stock	1.2 litres/2 pints
7.5 ml/1½ tsp	olive oil	15 ml/1 tbsp
½	small onion, peeled and chopped	1
1 small	garlic clove, peeled and crushed	1 large
100 g/4 oz	tomatoes, skinned and chopped	225 g/8 oz
2.5 ml/½ tsp	chopped fresh mixed herbs	5 ml/1 tsp
	salt and freshly ground black pepper	
7 g/¼ oz	butter	15 g/½ oz
	grated Parmesan cheese, to serve	

For one ——

* Place the fresh wholewheat spaghetti in a large shallow rectangular heatproof dish or casserole. Add the boiling stock, cover and microwave on HIGH for 4 minutes. Leave to stand, covered, while preparing the sauce.
* Place the oil in a bowl with the onion and garlic. Cover and microwave on HIGH for 1 minute.
* Stir in the tomatoes, herbs and salt and pepper to taste, blending well. Cover and microwave on HIGH for 1-1½ minutes, stirring once.
* Drain the spaghetti and toss in the butter. Place on a serving dish and spoon over the sauce. Serve at once sprinkled with grated Parmesan cheese.

For two ——

* Place the fresh wholewheat spaghetti in a large shallow rectangular heatproof dish or casserole. Add the boiling stock, cover and microwave on HIGH for 4 minutes. Leave to stand, covered, while preparing the sauce.
* Place the oil in a bowl with the onion and garlic. Cover and microwave on HIGH for 2 minutes.
* Stir in the tomatoes, herbs and salt and pepper to taste, blending well. Cover and microwave on HIGH for 2-3 minutes, stirring once.
* Drain the spaghetti and toss in the butter. Place on a serving dish and spoon over the sauce. Serve at once sprinkled with grated Parmesan cheese.

Stuffed redskins

Large, ripe, hand-sized beef tomatoes seem intended for stuffing. In this recipe they are filled fit-to-burst with rice, curried beans and mushrooms. Serve with a simple salad.

FOR ONE		FOR TWO
5 ml/1 tsp	oil	10 ml/2 tsp
½	small onion, peeled and chopped	1
50 g/2 oz	cooked rice	100 g/4 oz
5 ml/1 tsp	tomato purée	10 ml/2 tsp
25 g/1 oz	button mushrooms, wiped and chopped	50 g/2 oz
	salt and freshly ground black pepper	
1	large beef tomato(es)	2
1 x 50-75 g/2-3 oz	canned curried beans	1 x 100-175 g/4-6 oz
	pinch of dried mixed herbs	

For one ———

* Place the oil and onion in a bowl. Cover and microwave on HIGH for 1½ minutes. Add the rice, blending well.
* Add the tomato purée, mushrooms and salt and pepper to taste, blending well. Cover and microwave on HIGH for 2 minutes, stirring once.
* Meanwhile, using a serrated knife, cut off and reserve the top of the tomato. Carefully scoop out and discard the seeds.
* Mix the rice with the curried beans and herbs, blending well. Spoon into the tomato case using the reserved top to make a lid and place in a shallow dish.
* Reduce the power setting and microwave on MEDIUM for 2-3 minutes until hot, bubbly and cooked. Serve at once with a salad.

For two ———

* Place the oil and onion in a bowl. Cover and microwave on HIGH for 2 minutes. Add the rice, blending well.
* Add the tomato purée, mushrooms and salt and pepper to taste, blending well. Cover and microwave on HIGH for 3-4 minutes, stirring once.
* Meanwhile, using a serrated knife cut off and reserve the tops of the tomatoes. Carefully scoop out and discard the seeds.

117

- Mix the rice with the curried beans and herbs, blending well. Spoon into the tomato cases using the reserved tops to make a lid and place in a shallow dish.
- Reduce the power setting and microwave on MEDIUM for 3-4 minutes until hot, bubbly and cooked. Serve at once with a salad.

Stuffed eggs Florentine

Stuffed hard-boiled eggs nesting on a bed of leaf spinach and topped with a savoury cheese sauce makes a delicious and economical main meal. Serve with fingers of warm toast.

FOR ONE		FOR TWO
100 g/4 oz	frozen leaf spinach	225 g/8 oz
	pinch of ground nutmeg	
2	hard-boiled eggs, shelled and halved lengthwise	4
25 g/1 oz	butter	50 g/2 oz
15 g/½ oz	chopped cooked mushrooms	25 g/1 oz
5 ml/1 tsp	chopped fresh parsley	10 ml/2 tsp
150 ml/¼ pint	hot Cheese sauce (see page 150)	300 ml/½ pint

For one ——

- Place the spinach in a small gratin dish. Sprinkle with a little ground nutmeg. Cover and microwave on HIGH for 3-4 minutes.
- Meanwhile, remove the yolks from the eggs and mix with the butter, mushrooms and parsley. Spoon the mixture back into the egg whites and sandwich together. Place on top of the spinach.
- Pour over the sauce and microwave on HIGH for 1 minute to reheat. Brown under a preheated grill if liked. Serve at once.

For two ——

- Place the spinach in a small gratin dish. Sprinkle with a little ground nutmeg. Cover and microwave on HIGH for 7-8 minutes.
- Meanwhile, remove the yolks from the eggs and mix with the butter, mushrooms and parsley. Spoon the mixture back into the egg whites and sandwich together. Place on top of the spinach.
- Pour over the sauce and microwave on HIGH for 1½-2 minutes to reheat. Brown under a preheated grill if liked. Serve at once.

Cook's tip

Frozen spinach is an ideal vegetable to cook in the microwave both as a vegetable accompaniment and as part of a cooked dish. It is much quicker and easier to use than fresh spinach.

Spanish omelette

A main-course omelette cooked with onion, pepper, tomatoes and potato. Serve with a seasonal green salad and crusty bread.

FOR ONE		FOR TWO
½	medium onion, peeled and finely chopped	1
½	small green pepper, cored, seeded and chopped	1
½	tomato, skinned, seeded and chopped	1
20 g/¾ oz	butter	40 g/1½ oz
½	large cooked potato, diced	1
2	eggs, beaten	4
20 ml/4 tsp	milk	45 ml/3 tbsp
	salt and freshly ground black pepper	

For one —

- ◆ Place the onion, pepper, tomato and 15 g/½ oz of the butter in a bowl. Cover and microwave on HIGH for 2 minutes. Add the potato, blending well.
- ◆ Mix the eggs with the milk and the salt and pepper to taste, blending well.
- ◆ Place the remaining butter in a 15-18 cm/6-7 inch pie plate and microwave on HIGH for ½ minute to melt. Swirl the butter over the plate to coat.
- ◆ Mix the egg mixture with the vegetable mixture and pour into the plate. Cover with pierced cling film and microwave on HIGH for 1 minute. Using a fork, move the cooked egg from the edge of the dish to the centre. Re-cover and microwave on HIGH for a further 1-1½ minutes. Allow to stand for 2 minutes until set. Serve at once.

For two —

- ◆ Place the onion, pepper, tomato and 25 g/1 oz of the butter in a bowl. Cover and microwave on HIGH for 3 minutes. Add the potato, blending well.
- ◆ Mix the eggs with the milk and the salt and pepper to taste, blending well.
- ◆ Place the remaining butter in a 25 cm/10 inch pie plate and microwave on HIGH for ¾-1 minute to melt. Swirl the butter over the plate to coat.

- Mix the egg mixture with the vegetable mixture and pour into the plate. Cover with pierced cling film and microwave on HIGH for 1½-2 minutes. Using a fork, move the cooked egg from the edge of the dish to the centre. Re-cover and microwave on HIGH for a further 1½-2¼ minutes. Allow to stand for 2 minutes until set. Serve at once.

Save and savour

Use any leftover ingredients for this Spanish Omelette but make sure that they are chopped evenly and neatly.

Vegetarian fajitas

I like to serve this spicy fajita mix of spicy peppers, beans and avocado in either tortilla 'boats' or 'pockets' and, depending upon their size, you may have one or two per portion. You can warm the tortillas in the microwave on HIGH for 15-30 seconds using a microwave cover and then fill your way – loaded with the bean mix and avocado and topped with soured cream and maybe extra coriander.

FOR ONE		FOR TWO
5 ml/1 tsp	oil	10 ml/2 tsp
100 g/4 oz	yellow and red pepper strips	225 g/8 oz
¼	red onion, sliced	½
½	garlic clove, crushed	1
1.25 ml/scant ¼ tsp	chilli powder	1.25 ml/¼ tsp
1.25 ml/scant ¼ tsp	ground cumin	1.25 ml/¼ tsp
1.25 ml/¼ tsp	smoked paprika	2.5 ml/scant ½ tsp
60 g/2½ oz	canned black beans	125 g/4½ oz
15 ml/1 tbsp	lime juice	30 ml/2 tbsp
15 ml/1 tbsp	chopped fresh coriander	30 ml/2 tbsp
¼	avocado, peeled and sliced	½
	salt and freshly ground black pepper	
1-2	tortilla boats or pockets (see intro)	2-4
	soured cream to serve	

For one ——

- Place the oil, peppers, red onion, garlic, chilli powder, cumin and paprika in a dish. Cover and microwave on HIGH for 3 minutes.
- Add the black beans, lime juice and coriander, mixing well. Microwave, covered, on HIGH for 30 seconds.

- Add the avocado with salt and pepper to taste. Cover and leave to stand for 1 minute. Reheat or warm the tortilla pockets or boats while the mixture is standing to warm through (see intro).
- Fill the warm boats or pockets with the bean mixture and serve topped with a little soured cream.

For two

- Place the oil, peppers, red onion, garlic, chilli powder, cumin and paprika in a dish. Cover and microwave on HIGH for 4-4½ minutes.
- Add the black beans, lime juice and coriander, mixing well. Microwave, covered, on HIGH for 45 seconds.
- Add the avocado with salt and pepper to taste. Cover and leave to stand for 1 minute. Reheat or warm the tortilla pockets or boats while the mixture is standing to warm through (see intro).
- Fill the warm boats or pockets with the bean mixture and serve topped with a little soured cream.

Simplest Thai green curry

The simple and short list of ingredients for this Thai green curry doesn't do justice to its complex flavour and satisfying taste. I used quick cook vermicelli rice noodles for it but you can use others although the cooking time will be different. I also used a mixture of frozen carrots, peas and green beans but again you can replace with whatever you like or have to hand.

FOR ONE		FOR TWO
125 g/4½ oz	coconut milk	250 ml/8 fl oz
5 ml/1 tsp	Thai green curry paste	10 ml/2 tsp
75 g /3 oz	frozen carrots, peas and green beans	175 g/6 oz
25 g/1 oz	vermicelli rice noodles	50 g/2 oz
15 ml/1 tbsp	lime juice	30 ml/2 tbsp
	salt and freshly ground black pepper	
15 ml/1 tbsp	chopped fresh coriander	30 ml/2 tbsp
	sliced red chilli to garnish, optional	

For one

- Place the coconut milk, curry paste, frozen vegetables, roughly broken noodles, lime juice and salt and pepper to taste in a dish, mixing well. Cover and microwave on HIGH for 2 minutes.

- Add 2 tbsp water and mix well. Re-cover and microwave on HIGH for 1½ minutes, or until the noodles are soft and cooked to your liking. Leave to stand, covered, for 2 minutes.
- Stir in the coriander and serve garnished with sliced red chilli if liked.

For two

- Place the coconut milk, curry paste, frozen vegetables, roughly broken noodles, lime juice and salt and pepper to taste in a dish, mixing well. Cover and microwave on HIGH for 3 minutes.
- Add 4 tbsp water and mix well. Re-cover and microwave on HIGH for 2½-3 minutes, or until the noodles are soft and cooked to your liking. Leave to stand, covered, for 2 minutes.
- Stir in the coriander and serve garnished with sliced red chilli if liked.

Deeply satisfying sweet potato and lentil dhal

I feel as though I could eat dhal almost every day but sometimes just on the side of a curry dish. This isn't a recipe for a side dhal – something much more of a one dish assembly that is deeply satisfying and comforting. My only personal stipulation is a spoonful of mango chutney alongside, but it is optional.

FOR ONE		FOR TWO
5 ml/1 tsp	sesame oil	10 ml/2 tsp
¼	red onion, chopped	½
½	garlic clove, crushed	1
5 ml/1 tsp	chopped root ginger	10 ml/2 tsp
1.25 ml/¼ tsp	chopped red chilli	2.5 ml/½ tsp
2.5 ml/½ tsp	turmeric	5 ml/1 tsp
2.5 ml/½ tsp	ground cumin	5 ml/1 tsp
100 g/4 oz	peeled sweet potato cubes	200 g/7 oz
60 g/2½ oz	red split lentils	125 g/4½ oz
250 ml/8 fl oz	hot vegetable stock	450 ml/15 fl oz
	salt and freshly ground black pepper	
20 g/¾ oz	spinach leaves	40 g/1½ oz
1	spring onion(s), chopped	2
	Thai basil sprigs to garnish	

For one ——

* Place the oil and red onion in a bowl and microwave, covered, on HIGH for 2 minutes.
* Add the garlic, ginger, chilli, turmeric and cumin and stir well. Microwave on HIGH for ½ minute.
* Add the sweet potato, lentils, stock and salt and pepper to taste, mixing well. Cover and microwave on HIGH for 4½ minutes.
* Stir well, re-cover then microwave on MEDIUM for 5 minutes or until the lentils are just tender and the potato is cooked but still firm.
* Stir in the spinach mixing well. Re-cover and microwave on HIGH for ½ minute so that it wilts. Leave to stand for 1 minute before serving topped with the spring onion and scattered with torn basil leaves.

For two ——

* Place the oil and red onion in a bowl and microwave, covered, on HIGH for 2½ minutes.
* Add the garlic, ginger, chilli, turmeric and cumin and stir well. Microwave on HIGH for ¾ minute.
* Add the sweet potato, lentils, stock and salt and pepper to taste, mixing well. Cover and microwave on HIGH for 6-7 minutes.
* Stir well, re-cover then microwave on MEDIUM for 7-8 minutes or until the lentils are just tender and the potato is cooked but still firm.
* Stir in the spinach mixing well. Re-cover and microwave on HIGH for ½-1 minute so that it wilts. Leave to stand for 1 minute before serving topped with the spring onion and scattered with torn basil leaves.

Springtime risotto

Making risotto on the hob can be time-consuming – all that stirring! But the microwave makes light work of it so is a great way of making this very moreish rice dish. This spring time or 'primavera' risotto is gorgeous with its asparagus, pea and bean additions plus a morsel or two of soft creamy goat's cheese.

FOR ONE		FOR TWO
75 g/3 oz	risotto or Arborio rice	175 g/6 oz
350 ml/12 fl oz	hot vegetable stock	700 ml/18 fl oz
125 g/4 oz	frozen pea and bean mix	250 g/9 oz
25 g/1 oz	fresh asparagus tips, halved	50 g/2 oz
40 g/1½ oz	soft goat's cheese, diced	75 g/3 oz
	salt and freshly ground black pepper	
15 ml/1 tbsp	chopped fresh mint	30 ml/2 tbsp

For one

- Place the rice and half of the stock in a dish. Cover and microwave on HIGH for 6 minutes.
- Add half of the remaining stock, stirring well. Re-cover and microwave on HIGH for 3 minutes.
- Add the remaining stock, pea and bean mix and asparagus, mixing well. Re-cover and microwave on HIGH for 4-5 minutes.
- Stir in the cheese, seasoning to taste and mint. Cover and leave to stand for 2 minutes before serving.

For two

- Place the rice and half of the stock in a dish. Cover and microwave on HIGH for 9 minutes.
- Add half of the remaining stock, stirring well. Re-cover and microwave on HIGH for 5 minutes.
- Add the remaining stock, pea and bean mix and asparagus, mixing well. Re-cover and microwave on HIGH for 6-7 minutes.
- Stir in the cheese, seasoning to taste and mint. Cover and leave to stand for 2 minutes before serving.

Butternut squash and sage risotto

It's easy to eat well and speedily if you employ the microwave to do the hard slog and this recipe for a risotto with butternut squash, spinach and sage is easy, quick and delicious. You can buy ready prepared butternut squash if liked to cut down on prep time but the microwave will even help with this if using a whole unpeeled squash. To peel, pierce the squash with a fork, slice the top and bottom off and microwave on HIGH for 3-4 minutes. Allow it to cool slightly then remove the skin easily with a vegetable peeler.

FOR ONE		FOR TWO
250 ml/8 fl oz	hot vegetable stock	500 ml/18 fl oz
½	onion, chopped	1
1.25 ml/¼ tsp	dried sage	2.5 ml/½ tsp
75 g/3 oz	risotto or Arborio rice	150 g/5 oz
100 g/4 oz	peeled and cubed butternut squash	200 g/7 oz
1 handful	fresh spinach leaves	2 handfuls
	salt and freshly ground black pepper	
	grated Parmesan cheese to serve	

For one —

- Place half of the stock in a dish with the onion, sage and rice. Stir well then cover and microwave on HIGH for 4 minutes.
- Remove from the microwave and stir in the squash, spinach and remaining stock, mixing well. Re-cover and microwave on HIGH for 7-8 minutes or until most of the stock has been absorbed and the rice is tender.
- Stir well, add seasoning to taste and leave to stand, covered, for 3 minutes before serving sprinkled with Parmesan cheese.

For two —

- Place half of the stock in a dish with the onion, sage and rice. Stir well then cover and microwave on HIGH for 5-6 minutes.
- Remove from the microwave and stir in the squash, spinach and remaining stock, mixing well. Re-cover and microwave on HIGH for 10-11 minutes or until most of the stock has been absorbed and the rice is tender.
- Stir well, add seasoning to taste and leave to stand, covered, for 3 minutes before serving sprinkled with Parmesan cheese.

VEGETABLES, SALADS AND SIDE DISHES

Cabbage in soured cream mushroom sauce

Crunchy white cabbage served with a tangy mushroom sauce is delicious with almost any roast meat or game.

FOR ONE		FOR TWO
100 g/4 oz	white cabbage, cut into small wedges	225 g/8 oz
10 ml/2 tsp	water	20 ml/4 tsp
1	recipe hot Soured Cream Mushroom Sauce (see page 155)	1

For one —

* Place the cabbage and water in a bowl. Cover and microwave on HIGH for 2½-3½ minutes until tender, stirring gently once.
* Drain thoroughly. Spoon over the hot sauce and microwave on HIGH for ½ minute. Serve hot.

For two —

* Place the cabbage and water in a bowl. Cover and microwave on HIGH for 5-5½ minutes until tender, stirring gently once.
* Drain thoroughly. Spoon over the hot sauce and microwave on HIGH for ¾ minute. Serve hot.

Fantail lemon courgettes

These sliced and fanned courgettes look stunning and are very easy to do. Take care not to damage them during cooking when stirring or re-arranging.

FOR ONE		FOR TWO
2	medium courgettes	4
7 g/¼ oz	butter	15 g/½ oz
2.5 ml/½ tsp	finely grated lemon rind	5 ml/1 tsp
	salt and freshly ground white pepper	

For one ———

* Top and tail the courgettes, then thinly slice from one end almost to the other to make several thin layers. Gently prise the layers apart and open out to make a fan shape.
* Place in a shallow dish, dot with the butter, sprinkle with the lemon rind and season with salt and pepper to taste. Cover and microwave on HIGH for 1½-2 minutes, stirring or re-arranging once.

For two ———

* Top and tail the courgettes, then thinly slice from one end almost to the other to make several thin layers. Gently prise the layers apart and open out to make a fan shape.
* Place in a shallow dish, dot with the butter, sprinkle with the lemon rind and season with salt and pepper to taste. Cover and microwave on HIGH for 3-4 minutes, stirring or re-arranging once.

Cidered red cabbage and apple

A family favourite that I first tasted at Marden Fruit Show in Kent where top apple growers meet in friendly rivalry to compete for the best fruit awards.

FOR ONE		FOR TWO
150 g/5 oz	red cabbage, shredded	275 g/10 oz
7.5 ml/1½ tsp	cider or apple juice	15 ml/1 tbsp
½	large cooking apple, peeled, cored and finely sliced	1
	pinch of ground cloves	
2.5 ml/½ tsp	cider vinegar	5 ml/1 tsp
2.5 ml/½ tsp	brown sugar	5 ml/1 tsp
2.5 ml/½ tsp	redcurrant or quince jelly	5 ml/1 tsp
7 g/¼ oz	butter	15 g/½ oz

For one ———

* Place the cabbage, cider or apple juice and apple in a bowl. Cover and microwave on HIGH for 4-5 minutes, stirring once.
* Add the cloves, cider vinegar, sugar, jelly and butter, blending well. Cover and microwave on HIGH for ¾-1 minute, stirring once. Serve hot.

For two ———

* Place the cabbage, cider or apple juice and apple in a bowl. Cover and microwave on HIGH for 8-9 minutes, stirring once.
* Add the cloves, cider vinegar, sugar, jelly and butter, blending well. Cover and microwave on HIGH for 1-1½ minutes, stirring once. Serve hot.

Freezability

Cidered Red Cabbage and Apple will freeze well for up to 3 months. Defrost and reheat on HIGH for 4 minutes (for one) and 8 minutes (for two), stirring once.

Buttery lemon cabbage

Crisp and flavoursome, simple white cabbage is lifted from the humble to the luxury class when cooked with lemon and butter.

FOR ONE		FOR TWO
100 g/4 oz	white cabbage, finely shredded	225 g/8 oz
2.5 ml/½ tsp	finely grated lemon rind	5 ml/1 tsp
10 ml/2 tsp	lemon juice	20 ml/4 tsp
15 g/½ oz	butter	25 g/1 oz
30 ml/2 tbsp	chicken stock	60 ml/4 tbsp
	salt and freshly ground black pepper	

For one ——

◆ Place the cabbage, lemon rind, lemon juice, butter, stock and salt and pepper to taste in a bowl.

◆ Cover and microwave on HIGH for 2½-3½ minutes until tender, stirring once. Leave to stand for 3 minutes before serving.

For two ——

◆ Place the cabbage, lemon rind, lemon juice, butter, stock and salt and pepper to taste in a bowl.

◆ Cover and microwave on HIGH for 5-5½ minutes until tender, stirring once. Leave to stand for 3 minutes before serving.

Ratatouille

Colourful, exotic and flavoursome ratatouille is delicious served with pork or poultry. Alternatively serve chilled as a starter with crusty bread.

FOR ONE		FOR TWO
5 ml/1 tsp	oil	10 ml/2 tsp
½	small onion, peeled and chopped	1
½	garlic clove, peeled and crushed	1
½	green pepper, cored, seeded and sliced	1
75 g/3 oz	tomatoes, skinned and sliced	175 g/6 oz
100 g/4 oz	courgettes, topped, tailed and sliced	225 g/8 oz
15 g/½ oz	mushrooms, wiped and chopped	25 g/1 oz
1.25 ml/¼ tsp	dried thyme	2.5 ml/½ tsp
7.5 ml/1½ tsp	tomato purée	15 ml/1 tbsp
	salt and freshly ground black pepper	

For one

- Place the oil, onion, garlic and green pepper in a bowl. Cover and microwave on HIGH for 2½ minutes, stirring once.
- Add the tomatoes, courgettes, mushrooms, thyme, tomato purée and salt and pepper to taste, blending well. Cover and microwave on HIGH for 4-5 minutes, stirring twice. Serve hot or cold.

For two

- Place the oil, onion, garlic and green pepper in a bowl. Cover and microwave on HIGH for 4 minutes, stirring once.
- Add the tomatoes, courgettes, mushrooms, thyme, tomato purée and salt and pepper to taste, blending well. Cover and microwave on HIGH for 8-10 minutes, stirring twice. Serve hot or cold.

Freezability

Ratatouille will freeze well for up to 2 months. Cook and reheat from frozen – 1 portion should be cooked on DEFROST for 5 minutes then on HIGH for 2-3 minutes, stirring twice; 2 portions should be cooked on DEFROST for 10 minutes then on HIGH for 4-5 minutes, stirring twice.

Fennel and tomatoes

Fennel is a delicious vegetable that tastes rather like celery but stronger. Here it is joined with tomatoes, onion, garlic and parsley to make a tasty vegetable accompaniment.

FOR ONE		FOR TWO
½	fennel bulb, washed, trimmed and cut into quarters	1
30 ml/2 tbsp	water	60 ml/4 tbsp
1 x 225 g/8 oz	can peeled tomatoes, drained and coarsely chopped	1 x 398 g/14 oz
½	small onion, peeled and finely chopped	1
1.25 ml/¼ tsp	garlic purée	2.5 ml/½ tsp
5 ml/1 tsp	chopped fresh parsley	10 ml/2 tsp
	salt and freshly ground black pepper	

For one

- Place the fennel in a dish with the water. Cover and microwave on HIGH for 2½-3 minutes.
- Drain thoroughly and add the tomatoes, onion, garlic, parsley, salt and pepper to taste, blending well. Cover and microwave on HIGH for 5-6 minutes, stirring once.
- Allow to stand, covered, for 5 minutes before serving.

For two

- Place the fennel in a dish with the water. Cover and microwave on HIGH for 5 minutes.
- Drain thoroughly and add the tomatoes, onion, garlic, parsley, salt and pepper to taste, blending well. Cover and microwave on HIGH for 10 minutes, stirring once.
- Allow to stand, covered, for 5 minutes before serving.

Mangetout à la Française

A variation on a classic theme, mangetout are used in this delicious vegetable accompaniment instead of the traditional petit pois.

FOR ONE		FOR TWO
7 g/¼ oz	butter	15 g/½ oz
2	spring onions, thickly sliced	4
100 g/4 oz	mangetout, topped and tailed	225 g/8 oz
60 ml/4 tbsp	chicken stock	120 ml/4 fl oz
2.5 ml/½ tsp	chopped fresh mixed herbs	5 ml/1 tsp
	pinch of salt	
2.5 ml/½ tsp	cornflour	5 ml/1 tsp
1	small lettuce heart(s), quartered	2
15 ml/1 tbsp	double cream	30 ml/2 tbsp

For one

- Place the butter and spring onions in a bowl. Cover and microwave on HIGH for ½ minute.
- Add the mangetout, chicken stock and herbs, blending well. Cover and microwave on HIGH for 1½-2 minutes, stirring once.

- Mix the salt with the cornflour and enough water to make a smooth paste. Stir into the mangetout mixture, blending well. Cover and microwave on HIGH for ½ minute, stirring once.
- Add the lettuce heart and cream, blending well. Cover and microwave on HIGH for ¼-½ minute until the lettuce is just cooked but not limp. Serve at once.

For two ——

- Place the butter and spring onions in a bowl. Cover and microwave on HIGH for 1 minute.
- Add the mangetout, chicken stock and herbs, blending well. Cover and microwave on HIGH for 3-3½ minutes, stirring once.
- Mix the salt with the cornflour and enough water to make a smooth paste. Stir into the mangetout mixture, blending well. Cover and microwave on HIGH for ¾-1 minute, stirring once.
- Add the lettuce hearts and cream, blending well. Cover and microwave on HIGH for ½-¾ minute until the lettuce is just cooked but not limp. Serve at once.

Broccoli and ham in cheese sauce

When you want a quick, tasty meal in a hurry this savoury vegetable dish will fit the bill. Use smoked cheese in the cheese sauce for an unusual flavour.

FOR ONE		FOR TWO
1	large frozen broccoli spear(s)	2
1	slice(s) cooked ham	2
1	recipe hot Cheese Sauce (see page 150)	1
15 g/½ oz	grated cheese	25 g/1 oz

For one ——

- Place the broccoli in a dish. Cover and microwave on HIGH for 2 minutes until cooked. Drain if necessary.
- Roll the broccoli spear in the ham and place in a dish.
- Pour over the sauce and sprinkle with the cheese. Microwave on HIGH for 2-2½ minutes until hot and bubbly. Serve hot.

For two —

* Place the broccoli in a dish. Cover and microwave on HIGH for 3-4 minutes until cooked. Drain if necessary.
* Roll the broccoli spears in the ham and place in a dish.
* Pour over the sauce and sprinkle with the cheese. Microwave on HIGH for 4-4½ minutes until hot and bubbly. Serve hot.

Chinese stir fry vegetables

It is essential to use a browning dish in the preparation of this recipe because a hot surface is needed to sizzle and sear the cut vegetables.

FOR ONE		FOR TWO
5 ml/1 tsp	sesame oil	10 ml/2 tsp
¼	small onion, peeled and sliced	½
½	small red pepper, cored, seeded and sliced	1
1	small courgette(s), cut into thin julienne strips	2
1	carrot(s), peeled and cut into thin julienne strips	2
2.5 ml/½ tsp	finely chopped fresh root ginger	5 ml/1 tsp
25 g/1 oz	button mushrooms, wiped and sliced	50 g/2 oz
1.25 ml/¼ tsp	cornflour	2.5 ml/½ tsp
7.5 ml/1½ tsp	soy sauce	15 ml/1 tbsp
7.5 ml/1½ tsp	dry sherry	15 ml/1 tbsp
	pinch of Chinese 5 spice powder	

For one —

* Preheat a browning dish on HIGH for 8 minutes or according to the manufacturer's instructions. Add the oil and swirl to coat the base of the dish. Microwave on HIGH for ½ minute.
* Add the onion, pepper, courgette, carrot and ginger, blending well. Microwave on HIGH for 2 minutes, stirring twice.
* Add the mushrooms, blending well. Microwave on HIGH for a further ½ minute.
* Blend the cornflour with the soy sauce, sherry and Chinese 5 spice powder. Stir into the vegetable mixture and microwave on HIGH for ½-¾ minute, stirring twice until the juices are boiling and thickened. Stir to coat the vegetables and serve at once.

For two ———

* Preheat a browning dish on HIGH for 8 minutes or according to the manufacturer's instructions. Add the oil and swirl to coat the base of the dish. Microwave on HIGH for ½ minute.
* Add the onion, pepper, courgettes, carrots and ginger, blending well. Microwave on HIGH for 3 minutes, stirring twice.
* Add the mushrooms, blending well. Microwave on HIGH for a further 1 minute.
* Blend the cornflour with the soy sauce, sherry and Chinese 5 spice powder. Stir into the vegetable mixture and microwave on HIGH for 1-1½ minutes, stirring twice until the juices are boiling and thickened. Stir to coat the vegetables and serve at once.

Cook's tip

When preparing Chinese stir fried vegetables for a special meal try cutting the vegetables into flower, fish, arrow, star or moon shapes using a sharp knife or small canapé cutters.

Lemon glazed carrots

These strips of carrot cooked in a citrus butter are delicious served with fish, game or poultry.

FOR ONE		FOR TWO
100 g/4 oz	young carrots, peeled and sliced diagonally into strips	225 g/8 oz
30 ml/2 tbsp	lemon juice	60 ml/ 4 tbsp
7 g/¼ oz	butter	15 g/½ oz
1.25 ml/¼ tsp	brown sugar	2.5 ml/½ tsp
1.25 ml/¼ tsp	finely grated lemon rind	2.5 ml/½ tsp
	salt and freshly ground black pepper	
	chopped fresh parsley, to garnish	

For one ———

* Place the carrots and lemon juice in a dish. Cover and microwave on HIGH for 3-4 minutes, stirring once. Drain thoroughly.
* Place the butter, sugar and lemon rind in a bowl and microwave on HIGH for ¼ minute.

- Add the carrots with salt and pepper to taste and toss well to coat in the butter mixture.
- Cover and microwave on HIGH for ¼-½ minute. Garnish with chopped parsley; serve hot.

For two ⎯⎯

- Place the carrots and lemon juice in a dish. Cover and microwave on HIGH for 7-8 minutes, stirring once. Drain thoroughly.
- Place the butter, sugar and lemon rind in a bowl and microwave on HIGH for ½ minute.
- Add the carrots with salt and pepper to taste and toss well to coat in the butter mixture.
- Cover and microwave on HIGH for ½-1 minute. Garnish with chopped parsley; serve hot.

Cauliflower cheese

A tasty vegetable accompaniment which can also become a quick supper dish – with a little chopped cooked ham.

FOR ONE		FOR TWO
175 g/6 oz	cauliflower florets	350 g/12 oz
45 ml/3 tbsp	water	90 ml/6 tbsp
	pinch of salt	
150 ml/¼ pint	hot Cheese Sauce (see page 150)	300 ml/½ pint
15 ml/1 tbsp	grated cheese	30 ml/2 tbsp
	sweet paprika	

For one ⎯⎯

- Place the cauliflower florets, water and a pinch of salt in a bowl. Cover and microwave on HIGH for 4-5 minutes until tender, stirring once.
- Drain thoroughly and place in a serving dish. Spoon over the hot sauce, sprinkle with the cheese and a little paprika. Microwave on HIGH for 1 minute. Brown under a preheated grill, if liked.

For two ——

* Place the cauliflower florets, water and a pinch of salt in a bowl. Cover and microwave on HIGH for 7-8 minutes until tender, stirring once.
* Drain thoroughly and place in a serving dish. Spoon over the hot sauce, sprinkle with the cheese and a little paprika. Microwave on HIGH for 1½-2 minutes. Brown under a preheated grill, if liked.

Cauliflower Bombay style

I always want a few side dishes to my main meal curry and this is a favourite one, but in truth it makes a good main meal option in itself – I might well increase the quantities if serving that way. I would also drizzle with a little yogurt and accompany with some mango chutney to add additional interest and flavours.

FOR ONE		FOR TWO
15 ml/1 tbsp	oil	30 ml/2 tbsp
75 g/3 oz	small cauliflower florets	175 g/6 oz
15 ml/1 tbsp	red onion, chopped	30 ml/2 tbsp
1	garlic clove(s), crushed	2
7.5 ml/1½ tsp	root ginger, grated	15 ml/1 tbsp
	salt and freshly ground black pepper	
40 g/1½ oz	cooked chickpeas	75 g/3 oz
30 ml/2 tbsp	frozen peas	60 ml/4 tbsp
60 ml/4 tbsp	chopped tomatoes	120 ml/8 tbsp
7.5 ml/1½ tsp	butter	15 ml/1 tbsp
2.5 ml/½ tsp	mild chilli powder	5 ml/1 tsp
2.5 ml/½ tsp	turmeric	5 ml/1 tsp
5 ml/1 tsp	garam masala	10 ml/2 tsp
1.25 ml/¼ tsp	ground cumin	2.5 ml/½ tsp
2.5 ml/½ tsp	nigella seeds	5 ml/1 tsp
15 ml/1 tbsp	vegetable stock	30 ml/2 tbsp
5 ml/1 tsp	lemon juice	10 ml/2 tsp
	fresh coriander, chopped, to garnish (optional)	

For one ——

* Place the oil, cauliflower florets, onion, garlic, ginger and seasoning to taste in a dish. Microwave, uncovered, on HIGH for 3½ minutes.
* Add the chickpeas, frozen peas, tomatoes, butter, chilli powder, turmeric, garam masala, cumin, nigella seeds and stock then mix well to combine. Cover and microwave on HIGH for 2½ minutes.

- Remove from the microwave, uncover and stir to mix. Microwave, uncovered, on HIGH for a further 1¼-1½ minutes. Add the lemon juice, mix well then cover and leave to stand for 1 minute before serving sprinkled with chopped coriander if liked.

For two

- Place the oil, cauliflower florets, onion, garlic, ginger and seasoning to taste in a dish. Microwave, uncovered, on HIGH for 5½-6 minutes.
- Add the chickpeas, frozen peas, tomatoes, butter, chilli powder, turmeric, garam masala, cumin, nigella seeds and stock then mix well to combine. Cover and microwave on HIGH for 3½-4 minutes.
- Remove from the microwave, uncover and stir to mix. Microwave, uncovered, on HIGH for a further 2-2½ minutes. Add the lemon juice, mix well then cover and leave to stand for 1 minute before serving sprinkled with chopped coriander if liked.

Salads

Poppy seed and pine nut potato salad

A new potato salad mixed with crunchy poppy seeds and pine nuts in a light creamy dressing.

FOR ONE		FOR TWO
100 g/4 oz	new potatoes, scrubbed and cut into bite-sized chunks	225 g/8 oz
¼	small onion, peeled and chopped	½
15 ml/1 tbsp	water	30 ml/2 tbsp
15 ml/1 tbsp	mayonnaise	30 ml/2 tbsp
5 ml/1 tsp	soured cream or natural yogurt	10 ml/2 tsp
	salt and freshly ground black pepper	
15 g/½ oz	pine nuts, toasted	25 g/1 oz
5 ml/1 tsp	chopped fresh parsley	10 ml/2 tsp
2.5 ml/½ tsp	poppy seeds	5 ml/1 tsp

For one

- Place the potatoes, onion and water in a bowl. Cover and microwave on HIGH for 3 minutes, stirring once. Leave to stand for 2 minutes then drain thoroughly.
- Mix the mayonnaise with the soured cream or yogurt and salt and pepper to taste. Stir into the potato mixture. Fold in the pine nuts and parsley, blending well.
- Sprinkle with the poppy seeds and serve hot or cold.

For two

- Place the potatoes, onion and water in a bowl. Cover and microwave on HIGH for 6 minutes, stirring once. Leave to stand for 2 minutes then drain thoroughly.
- Mix the mayonnaise with the soured cream or yogurt and salt and pepper to taste. Stir into the potato mixture. Fold in the pine nuts and parsley, blending well.
- Sprinkle with the poppy seeds and serve hot or cold.

Curried rice, chicken and bean salad

Cooked chicken or canned blackeye beans are used in this fruity rice salad but cooked flageolet, cannellini or haricot beans could be used instead.

FOR ONE		FOR TWO
25 g/1 oz	long-grain white rice	50 g/2 oz
150 ml/¼ pint	boiling water	300 ml/½ pint
100 g/4 oz	cooked or canned blackeye beans	225 g/8 oz
15 g/½ oz	sultanas	25 g/1 oz
25 g/1 oz	mushrooms, sliced	50 g/2 oz
1	small celery stick(s), scrubbed and sliced	2
¼	red pepper, cored, seeded and chopped	½
15 g/½ oz	dried apricots, chopped	25 g/1 oz
75 g/3 oz	cooked chicken, skinned and chopped	175 g/6 oz
DRESSING		
25 ml/5 tsp	mayonnaise	45 ml/3 tbsp
2.5 ml/½ tsp	curry paste	5 ml/1 tsp
2.5 ml/½ tsp	mango chutney	5 ml/1 tsp
	salt and freshly ground black pepper	

For one ──

- ◆ Place the rice and water in a bowl. Cover and microwave on HIGH for 3 minutes. Reduce the power setting and microwave on MEDIUM for 12 minutes, stirring once. Leave to stand for 5 minutes. Drain if necessary and refresh under cold water.
- ◆ Mix the rice with the beans, sultanas, mushrooms, celery, pepper, apricots and chicken, blending well.
- ◆ To make the dressing, blend the mayonnaise with the curry paste, mango chutney and salt and pepper.
- ◆ Add the dressing to the salad and toss well to mix.

For two ──

- ◆ Place the rice and water in a bowl. Cover and microwave on HIGH for 3 minutes. Reduce the power setting and microwave on MEDIUM for 12 minutes, stirring once. Leave to stand for 5 minutes. Drain if necessary and refresh under cold water.
- ◆ Mix the rice with the beans, sultanas, mushrooms, celery, pepper, apricots and chicken, blending well.
- ◆ To make the dressing, blend the mayonnaise with the curry paste, mango chutney and salt and pepper.
- ◆ Add the dressing to the salad and toss well to mix.

Potato, bean and dill pickle salad

This Swedish style salad is delicious served with wafer thin slices of rare roast beef or spiced ham.

FOR ONE		FOR TWO
175 g/6 oz	small new potatoes, scrubbed	350 g/12 oz
45 ml/3 tbsp	water	90 ml/6 tbsp
50 g/2 oz	cooked red kidney beans	100 g/4 oz
¼	small onion, peeled and chopped	½
½	dill pickle, finely chopped	1
	DRESSING	
15 ml/1 tbsp	double cream	30 ml/2 tbsp
7.5 ml/1½ tsp	mayonnaise	15 ml/1 tbsp
2.5 ml/½ tsp	Dijon mustard	5 ml/1 tsp
	salt and freshly ground black pepper	

For one ——

* Place the potatoes and water in a bowl. Cover and microwave on HIGH for 5-6 minutes until tender. Drain then cut into bite-sized pieces. Allow to cool.
* Mix the potatoes with the beans, onion and dill pickle.
* To make the dressing, blend the cream with the mayonnaise, mustard and salt and pepper to taste.
* Add the dressing to the salad and toss well to mix. Serve lightly chilled.

For two ——

* Place the potatoes and water in a bowl. Cover and microwave on HIGH for 9-10 minutes until tender. Drain then cut into bite-sized pieces. Allow to cool.
* Mix the potatoes with the beans, onion and dill pickle.
* To make the dressing, blend the cream with the mayonnaise, mustard and salt and pepper to taste.
* Add the dressing to the salad and toss well to mix. Serve lightly chilled.

Spinach and bacon salad

It is essential to use only young tender spinach leaves for this salad, older leaves are too bitter.

FOR ONE		FOR TWO
100 g/4 oz	young spinach leaves	225 g/8 oz
40 g/1½ oz	back bacon, rinded	75 g/3 oz
½	small green pepper, cored, seeded and sliced	1
1	hard-boiled egg(s), shelled and quartered	2
30 ml/2 tbsp	French dressing	60 ml/4 tbsp
	snipped fresh chives, to garnish	

For one ——

* Strip the spinach leaves from their stems, wash thoroughly and dry. Place in a serving bowl.
* Place the bacon on a plate, cover with absorbent kitchen towel and microwave on HIGH for 2-3 minutes until crisp. Cool then crumble coarsely.
* Add the bacon, pepper and hard-boiled egg to the spinach. Pour over the dressing and toss lightly to mix.
* Garnish with snipped chives and serve at once.

For two

- Strip the spinach leaves from their stems, wash thoroughly and dry. Place in a serving bowl.
- Place the bacon on a plate, cover with absorbent kitchen towel and microwave on HIGH for 3½-4½ minutes until crisp. Cool then crumble coarsely.
- Add the bacon, pepper and hard-boiled eggs to the spinach. Pour over the dressing and toss lightly to mix.
- Garnish with snipped chives and serve at once.

Chicken papaya salad

This salad is deceptively hot and spicy. Serve as a main dish with corn chips or crisp crackers.

FOR ONE		FOR TWO
1 x 100 g/4 oz	boneless chicken breasts	2 x 100 g/4 oz
½	small red pepper, cored, seeded and sliced	1
½	small green pepper, cored, seeded and sliced	1
½	papaya, peeled, halved, seeded and sliced	1
½	small green chilli, seeded and very finely chopped	1
30 ml/2 tbsp	mayonnaise	60 ml/4 tbsp
15 ml/1 tbsp	soured cream	30 ml/2 tbsp

For one

- Place the chicken on a plate. Cover and microwave on HIGH for 2-2½ minutes until tender and cooked. Leave to stand until cool then remove and discard the skin. Cut the flesh into thin strips.
- Mix the chicken with the red pepper, green pepper and papaya.
- Mix the chilli with the mayonnaise and soured cream.
- Fold into the chicken mixture and chill for at least 1 hour to allow the flavours to blend. Serve lightly chilled.

For two

- Place the chicken on a plate. Cover and microwave on HIGH for 4-5 minutes until tender and cooked. Leave to stand until cool then remove and discard the skin. Cut the flesh into thin strips.
- Mix the chicken with the red pepper, green pepper and papaya.

- Mix the chilli with the mayonnaise and soured cream.
- Fold into the chicken mixture and chill for at least 1 hour to allow the flavours to blend. Serve lightly chilled.

Hi-Fi salad

The sesame seeds give an unexpected crunchy finish to this wholesome high fibre side salad.

FOR ONE		FOR TWO
5 ml/1 tsp	sesame seeds	10 ml/2 tsp
2.5 ml/½ tsp	oil	5 ml/1 tsp
25 g/1 oz	brown rice	50 g/2 oz
300 ml/½ pint	boiling water	450 ml/¾ pint
50 g/2 oz	fresh or canned sweetcorn kernels	100 g/4 oz
2	spring onions, trimmed and sliced	4
1	celery stick(s), scrubbed and sliced	2
15 g/½ oz	medium carrot, grated	25 g/1 oz
15 ml/1 tbsp	mayonnaise	30 ml/2 tbsp
	salt and freshly ground black pepper	

For one ——

- Place the sesame seeds and oil in a small bowl and microwave on HIGH for ½-1 minute until golden. Drain on absorbent kitchen towel.
- Place the rice and water in a bowl. Cover and microwave on HIGH for 5 minutes. Reduce the power setting and microwave on MEDIUM for 12-15 minutes, stirring once. Leave to stand for 5-10 minutes. Drain and refresh under cold water.
- Mix the rice with the sweetcorn, spring onions, celery, carrot, mayonnaise and salt and pepper. Serve cold sprinkled with the sesame seeds.

For two ——

- Place the sesame seeds and oil in a small bowl and microwave on HIGH for ¾-1½ minutes until golden. Drain on absorbent kitchen towel.
- Place the rice and water in a bowl. Cover and microwave on HIGH for 5 minutes. Reduce the power setting and microwave on MEDIUM for 12-15 minutes, stirring once. Leave to stand for 5-10 minutes. Drain and refresh under cold water.
- Mix the rice with the sweetcorn, spring onions, celery, carrot, mayonnaise and salt and pepper. Serve cold sprinkled with the sesame seeds.

Side dishes

Middle Eastern jewelled couscous with feta

Plain couscous doesn't hold much sway flavour wise but combine it with tomatoes, aubergine, peas, spices, citrus zest and herbs, then add jewelled pomegranate seeds and flaked almonds, as they do in the Middle East, and you get a very moreish mouthful. Sprinkle with crumbled salty feta at the end and you get a fabulous vegetarian side dish.

FOR ONE		FOR TWO
15 ml/1 tbsp	olive oil	30 ml/2 tbsp
15 ml/1 tbsp	onion, chopped	30 ml/2 tbsp
1	garlic clove(s), crushed	2
50 g/2 oz	aubergine, chopped	100 g/4 oz
40 g/1½ oz	frozen peas	75 g/3 oz
2	cherry tomatoes, quartered	4
2.5 ml/½ tsp	ground paprika	5 ml/1 tsp
2.5 ml/½ tsp	ground cumin	5 ml/1 tsp
2.5 ml/½ tsp	orange or lemon zest, grated	5 ml/1 tsp
65 g/2½ oz	dry couscous	150 g/5 oz
100 ml/3½ fl oz	vegetable stock	200 ml/7 fl oz
	salt and freshly ground black pepper	
15 ml/1 tbsp	pomegranate seeds	30 ml/2 tbsp
15 ml/1 tbsp	flaked almonds, toasted	30 ml/2 tbsp
30 ml/2 tbsp	fresh coriander, chopped	60 ml/4 tbsp
25 g/1 oz	feta cheese, crumbled	50 g/2 oz

For one

- Place the oil, onion, garlic, aubergine, peas, tomatoes, paprika, cumin and citrus zest in a dish, mixing well. Microwave, uncovered, on HIGH, for 4-4½ minutes, until softened and lightly cooked.
- Add the couscous and stock with seasoning to taste, mixing well. Cover and microwave on HIGH for 1½ minutes then leave to stand for 1 minute.
- Break up the couscous grains with a fork, add the pomegranate seeds, almonds and coriander and mix well to distribute evenly. Serve sprinkled with the crumbled feta cheese.

For two —

* Place the oil, onion, garlic, aubergine, peas, tomatoes, paprika, cumin and citrus zest in a dish, mixing well. Microwave, uncovered, on HIGH, for 6½-7 minutes, until softened and lightly cooked.
* Add the couscous and stock with seasoning to taste, mixing well. Cover and microwave on HIGH for 2½ minutes then leave to stand for 1 minute.
* Break up the couscous grains with a fork, add the pomegranate seeds, almonds and coriander and mix well to distribute evenly. Serve sprinkled with the crumbled feta cheese.

Savoury rice

Rice makes the perfect accompaniment to many main meal dishes. However, when something a little more exciting than plain boiled rice is required – try this version.

FOR ONE		FOR TWO
15 g/½ oz	butter	25 g/1 oz
½	small onion, peeled and chopped	1
½	small red pepper, cored, seeded and sliced	1
1	celery stick(s), scrubbed and sliced	2
25 g/1 oz	long-grain white rice	50 g/2 oz
150 ml/¼ pint	boiling stock or water	300 ml/½ pint
	salt and freshly ground black pepper	
	pinch of ground turmeric (optional)	
25 g/1 oz	frozen peas	50 g/2 oz

For one —

* Place the butter, onion, red pepper and celery in a large bowl. Cover and microwave on HIGH for 3 minutes, stirring once.
* Add the rice, boiling stock or water, salt and pepper to taste and turmeric, if used, blending well. Cover and microwave on HIGH for 3 minutes.
* Reduce the power setting and microwave on MEDIUM for 12 minutes, stirring once.
* Add the peas and leave to stand, covered, for 5 minutes before serving.

For two ——

- Place the butter, onion, red pepper and celery in a large bowl. Cover and microwave on HIGH for 4-5 minutes, stirring once.
- Add the rice, boiling stock or water, salt and pepper to taste and turmeric, if used, blending well. Cover and microwave on HIGH for 3 minutes.
- Reduce the power setting and microwave on MEDIUM for 12 minutes, stirring once.
- Add the peas and leave to stand, covered, for 5 minutes before serving.

Creamed coconut and pine nut rice

This is the perfect rice accompaniment to serve with curries.

FOR ONE		FOR TWO
75 g/3 oz	long-grain white rice	175 g/6 oz
250 ml/8 fl oz	boiling water	450 ml/¾ pint
10 ml/2 tsp	creamed coconut	15 ml/1 tbsp
15 g/½ oz	toasted pine nuts	25 g/1 oz
	salt and freshly ground black pepper	

For one ——

- Place the rice and the water in a bowl. Cover and microwave on HIGH for 3 minutes. Reduce the power setting and microwave on MEDIUM for 12 minutes. Leave to stand, covered, for 5 minutes.
- Stir the coconut and the pine nuts and salt and pepper to taste into the rice, blending well. Cover and microwave on HIGH for 1 minute to reheat. Serve at once.

For two ——

- Place the rice and the water in a bowl. Cover and microwave on HIGH for 3 minutes. Reduce the power setting and microwave on MEDIUM for 12 minutes. Leave to stand, covered, for 5 minutes.
- Stir the coconut and the pine nuts and salt and pepper to taste into the rice, blending well. Cover and microwave on HIGH for 1½ minutes to reheat. Serve at once.

Creamy coconut and red lentil dhal

This recipe for dhal has become a real favourite and the additional bonus to the speed at which it cooks and the fantastic flavour it has, is the economy it brings too – a portion costs pennies rather than pounds. It's also an amazingly time-tolerant and a leave-it-to-cook type recipe. I like to serve with basmati rice but it's fabulous without – perhaps with a little Naan bread if you are especially hungry.

FOR ONE		FOR TWO
7.5 ml/1½ tsp	oil	15 ml/1 tbsp
3.75 ml/¾ tsp	cumin seeds	7.5 ml/1½ tsp
50 g/2 oz	chopped onion	100 g/4 oz
1	garlic clove(s), crushed	2
15 ml/1 tbsp	chopped root ginger	30 ml/2 tbsp
1.25 ml/¼ tsp	turmeric	2.5 ml/½ tsp
1.25 ml/¼ tsp	chilli powder	2.5 ml/½ tsp
50 g/2 oz	washed red split lentils	100 g/4 oz
100 g/4 oz	canned chopped tomatoes	225 g/8 oz
100 g/4 oz	coconut milk	225 g/8 oz
	salt and freshly ground black pepper	
15 ml/1 tbsp	lime juice	30 ml/2 tbsp
15 ml/1 tbsp	chopped fresh coriander	30 ml/2 tbsp

For one ⸺

- Place the oil and cumin seeds in a dish and microwave, uncovered, on HIGH for 1 minute.
- Stir in the onion, garlic, ginger, turmeric and chilli powder and microwave, uncovered, on HIGH for 1 minute.
- Add the lentils, tomatoes, coconut milk, salt and pepper to taste and 3 tbsp boiling water, mixing well. Cover and microwave on HIGH for 8 minutes.
- Remove from the microwave, add 3 further tbsp boiling water, mixing well. Re-cover and microwave on MEDIUM for 5 minutes. Leave to stand, covered, for 2 minutes.
- Stir in the lime juice and coriander to serve.

For two

- Place the oil and cumin seeds in a dish and microwave, uncovered, on HIGH for 1¼ minutes.
- Stir in the onion, garlic, ginger, turmeric and chilli powder and microwave, uncovered, on HIGH for 1½ minutes.
- Add the lentils, tomatoes, coconut milk, salt and pepper to taste and 6 tbsp boiling water, mixing well. Cover and microwave on HIGH for 11-12 minutes.
- Remove from the microwave, add 6 further tbsp boiling water, mixing well. Re-cover and microwave on MEDIUM for 8 minutes. Leave to stand, covered, for 2 minutes.
- Stir in the lime juice and coriander to serve.

Garlic bread rolls

A one and two portion variation of the typical French Stick Garlic Bread.

FOR ONE		FOR TWO
1	long finger-shaped crusty bread roll(s)	2
1	recipe Garlic Butter (see page 160)	1

For one

- Cut the bread roll in half and spread with the garlic butter. Sandwich together again.
- Wrap the roll in absorbent kitchen towel and microwave on HIGH for ¼-½ minute or until the butter has just melted and the bread is warm. Serve at once.

For two

- Cut the bread rolls in half and spread with the garlic butter. Sandwich together again.
- Wrap the rolls in absorbent kitchen towel and microwave on HIGH for ½-1 minute or until the butter has just melted and the bread is warm. Serve at once.

Crispy croutons

Crisp bread croutons make a delicious topping for soups and savoury dishes or, if tossed in a little sea salt and chopped fresh herbs, a delicious snack or cocktail nibble.

FOR ONE		FOR TWO
25 g/1 oz	butter	50 g/2 oz
1½	large slices of bread, crusts removed and cut into small cubes	3

For one ——

* ♦ Place the butter in a bowl and microwave on HIGH for ¾ minute to melt.
* ♦ Add the bread cubes and toss to coat, microwave on HIGH for ¾-1 minute. Stir well and microwave on HIGH for a further ¾ minute until golden and crisp. Drain on absorbent kitchen towel.

For two ——

* ♦ Place the butter in a bowl and microwave on HIGH for 1 minute to melt.
* ♦ Add the bread cubes and toss to coat, microwave on HIGH for 1½ minutes. Stir well and microwave on HIGH for a further 1½ minutes until golden and crisp. Drain on absorbent kitchen towel.

SAUCES, BUTTERS AND DRESSINGS

Basic white pouring sauce

FOR ONE		FOR TWO
15 g/½ oz	butter	25 g/1 oz
15 g/½ oz	plain flour	25 g/1 oz
150 ml/¼ pint	milk	300 ml/½ pint
	salt and freshly ground black pepper	

For one

- Place the butter in a jug and microwave on HIGH for ¼-½ minute to melt.
- Add the flour, blending well. Gradually add the milk and salt and pepper to taste.
- Microwave on HIGH for 1½-2 minutes, stirring 3 times until smooth and thickened. Use as required.

For two

- Place the butter in a jug and microwave on HIGH for ½ minute to melt.
- Add the flour, blending well. Gradually add the milk and salt and pepper to taste.
- Microwave on HIGH for 3½-4 minutes, stirring 3 times until smooth and thickened. Use as required.

Variations

BASIC WHITE COATING SAUCE

Prepare and cook as above but double the quantities of both butter and flour in each case.

CHEESE SAUCE

Prepare and cook as above then add 25 g/1 oz grated cheese and a pinch of mustard powder for every 150 ml/¼ pint milk used. Stir well to blend.

PARSLEY SAUCE

Prepare and cook as above then add 7.5 ml/1½ teaspoons chopped fresh parsley for every 150 ml/¼ pint milk used. Stir well to blend.

CAPER SAUCE

Prepare and cook as above then add 1½ teaspoons chopped capers and 1 teaspoon white wine vinegar for every 150 ml/¼ pint milk used. Stir well to blend.

Béchamel sauce

This rich, creamy sauce cooks quickly in the microwave and emerges velvety-smooth and lump free.

FOR ONE		FOR TWO
1	small onion, peeled	1
6	cloves	6
1	bay leaf	1
3	peppercorns	6
½	small carrot, peeled	1
150 ml/¼ pint	milk	300 ml/½ pint
15 g/½ oz	butter	25 g/1 oz
15 g/½ oz	flour	25 g/1 oz
	salt and freshly ground black pepper	

For one ——

- Stud the onion with the cloves and place in a bowl with the bay leaf, peppercorns, carrot and milk. Cover and microwave on DEFROST power for 5-6 minutes until hot.
- Place the butter in a jug and microwave on HIGH for ½ minute to melt. Stir in the flour, blending well. Gradually add the strained milk and salt and pepper to taste.
- Microwave on HIGH for 1-1¼ minutes until smooth and thickened, stirring twice. Use as required.

For two ——

- Stud the onion with the cloves and place in a bowl with the bay leaf, peppercorns, carrot and milk. Cover and microwave on DEFROST power for 10-11 minutes until hot.
- Place the butter in a jug and microwave on HIGH for ¾ minute to melt. Stir in the flour, blending well. Gradually add the strained milk and salt and pepper to taste.
- Microwave on HIGH for 1½-2 minutes until smooth and thickened, stirring twice. Use as required.

Variations

AURORE SAUCE

Prepare and cook as above then add 15 ml/1 tbsp tomato purée and a pinch of caster sugar for every 150 ml/¼ pint milk used. Stir well to blend.

TARRAGON SAUCE

Prepare and cook as above then add 7.5 ml/1½ tsp chopped fresh tarragon for every 150 ml/¼ pint milk used. Stir well to blend.

MORNAY SAUCE

Prepare and cook as above then add 15 g/½ oz each of grated Cheddar and Parmesan cheese and a little French mustard for every 150 ml/¼ pint milk used. Whisk until the cheese melts and the sauce is smooth.

Béarnaise sauce

It is essential to use a blender or food processor for this sauce. Serve with steaks, poached eggs on toast or cooked green vegetables.

FOR ONE		FOR TWO
2	small egg yolks (size 5 or 6)	4
3.75 ml/¾ tsp	white wine vinegar	7.5 ml/1½ tsp
3.75 ml/¾ tsp	dry white wine	7.5 ml/1½ tsp
	pinch chopped fresh or dried tarragon	
	salt and freshly ground black pepper	
40 g/1½ oz	butter	75 g/3 oz
7.5 ml/1½ tsp	very finely chopped onion	15 ml/1 tbsp

For one ——

- Place the egg yolks, wine vinegar, wine, tarragon and salt and pepper to taste in a blender. Process for about 3-5 seconds until smooth and blended.
- Place the butter and onion in a bowl. Cover and microwave on HIGH for ½-¾ minute until hot and bubbly.
- With the blender running on low speed, add the butter mixture to the egg yolk mixture in a steady stream until the sauce thickens.
- Pour into a serving bowl and microwave on MEDIUM for ½-1 minute until hot, thick and creamy, stirring three times. Serve at once.

For two ——

- Place the egg yolks, wine vinegar, wine, tarragon and salt and pepper to taste in a blender. Process for about 3-5 seconds until smooth and blended.
- Place the butter and onion in a bowl. Cover and microwave on HIGH for ¾-1¼ minutes until hot and bubbly.
- With the blender running on low speed, add the butter mixture to the egg yolk mixture in a steady stream until the sauce thickens.
- Pour into a serving bowl and microwave on MEDIUM for 1-2 minutes until hot, thick and creamy, stirring three times. Serve at once.

Hollandaise sauce

A velvety smooth sauce to serve hot with poached salmon, globe artichokes or cooked vegetables.

FOR ONE		FOR TWO
1	small egg yolk(s) (size 5 or 6)	2
7.5 ml/1½ tsp	lemon juice	15 ml/1 tbsp
	salt and freshly ground black pepper	
25 g/1 oz	butter	50 g/2 oz

For one —

- Place the egg yolks, lemon juice and salt and pepper to taste in a blender or small bowl and blend or whisk with a hand-held beater until frothy.
- Dice the butter and place in a jug. Cover and microwave on HIGH for ¾ minute to melt.
- Whisking vigorously or with the blender on high speed, slowly pour the butter into the egg mixture, blending or whisking until the sauce is very thick, smooth and creamy.
- Return to the jug and place in a bowl of hand-hot water (making sure the water level in the bowl is the same as the sauce level).
- Microwave uncovered, on LOW for 1½-1¾ minutes, stirring twice. Stir and serve at once.

For two —

- Place the egg yolks, lemon juice and salt and pepper to taste in a blender or small bowl and blend or whisk with a hand-held beater until frothy.
- Dice the butter and place in a jug. Cover and microwave on HIGH for 1-1¼ minutes to melt.
- Whisking vigorously or with the blender on high speed, slowly pour the butter into the egg mixture, blending or whisking until the sauce is very thick, smooth and creamy.
- Return to the jug and place in a bowl of hand-hot water (making sure the water level in the bowl is the same as the sauce level).
- Microwave uncovered, on LOW for 3-3½ minutes, stirring twice. Stir and serve at once.

Sweet and sour sauce

A must for chicken, pork and prawn sweet and sour dishes.

FOR ONE		FOR TWO
20 ml/4 tsp	vinegar	45 ml/3 tbsp
15 ml/1 tsp	sugar	30 ml/2 tbsp
15 ml/1 tsp	cornflour	30 ml/2 tbsp
15 ml/1 tsp	tomato purée	30 ml/2 tbsp
5 ml/1 tsp	soy sauce	10 ml/2 tsp
½ x 225 g/8 oz	can pineapple pieces in natural juice	1 x 225 g/8 oz
	small piece of cucumber, cut into thin julienne strips	

For one

- Place the vinegar, sugar, cornflour, tomato purée, soy sauce and pineapple juice (but not pieces) in a bowl, blending well.
- Microwave on HIGH for 1½ minutes, stirring twice until smooth and thickened.
- Add the pineapple pieces and cucumber, blending well. Microwave on HIGH for a further 1½-2 minutes, stirring once. Use as required.

For two

- Place the vinegar, sugar, cornflour, tomato purée, soy sauce and pineapple juice (but not pieces) in a bowl, blending well.
- Microwave on HIGH for 3 minutes, stirring twice until smooth and thickened.
- Add the pineapple pieces and cucumber, blending well. Microwave on HIGH for a further 3 minutes, stirring once. Use as required.

Soured cream mushroom sauce

This tangy sauce is perfect for serving with pork chops, veal escalopes, gammon, chicken or game birds.

FOR ONE		FOR TWO
15 g/½ oz	butter	25 g/1 oz
50 g/2 oz	button mushrooms, wiped and sliced	100 g/4 oz
20 g/¾ oz	flour	40 g/1½ oz
30 ml/2 tbsp	dry sherry	60 ml/4 tbsp
75 ml/5 tbsp	soured cream	150 ml/¼ pint
75 ml/5 tbsp	meat stock or cooked meat juices	150 ml/¼ pint
	salt and freshly ground black pepper	

For one ⸺

- Place the butter and mushrooms in a bowl. Cover and microwave on HIGH for 1½-2 minutes, stirring once.
- Add the flour, blending well. Microwave on HIGH for ¼ minute.
- Gradually add the sherry, soured cream, stock or meat juices and salt and pepper to taste, blending well.
- Reduce the power setting to MEDIUM and microwave for 4-5 minutes, stirring twice until creamy and thickened but do not allow to boil. Serve at once.

For two ⸺

- Place the butter and mushrooms in a bowl. Cover and microwave on HIGH for 3½ minutes, stirring once.
- Add the flour, blending well. Microwave on HIGH for ½ minute.
- Gradually add the sherry, soured cream, stock or meat juices and salt and pepper to taste, blending well.
- Reduce the power setting to MEDIUM and microwave for 8 minutes, stirring twice until creamy and thickened but do not allow to boil. Serve at once.

Barbecue sauce

To baste, coat or serve with plain cooked meats, fish and poultry, this sauce has just as good a flavour as a more complicated long-simmered version.

FOR ONE		FOR TWO
½	small onion, peeled and chopped	1
½	small garlic clove, peeled and crushed	1
75 ml/5 tbsp	tomato ketchup	150 ml/¼ pint
7.5 ml/1½ tsp	water	15 ml/1 tbsp
10 ml/2 tsp	red wine vinegar	20 ml/4 tsp
7.5 ml/1½ tsp	Worcestershire sauce	15 ml/1 tbsp
2.5 ml/½ tsp	soy sauce	5 ml/1 tsp
15 g/½ oz	brown sugar	25 g/1 oz
7.5 ml/1½ tsp	oil	15 ml/1 tbsp
2.5 ml/½ tsp	lemon juice	5 ml/1 tsp

For one ⸺

- Place the onion, garlic, tomato ketchup, water, vinegar, Worcestershire sauce, soy sauce, sugar, oil and lemon juice in a bowl, blending well.
- Cover and microwave on HIGH for 2-3 minutes, stirring twice.
- Leave to stand for 5 minutes. Use as required.

For two ⸺

- Place the onion, garlic, tomato ketchup, water, vinegar, Worcestershire sauce, soy sauce, sugar, oil and lemon juice in a bowl, blending well.
- Cover and microwave on HIGH for 4-4½ minutes, stirring twice.
- Leave to stand for 5 minutes. Use as required.

Tomato sauce

This vibrant tomato sauce is equally good with pasta, hamburgers or chicken. If a chunky sauce is preferred then do not purée.

FOR ONE		FOR TWO
7 g/¼ oz	butter	15 g/½ oz
¼	small onion, peeled and chopped	½
7 g/¼ oz	flour	15 g/½ oz
100 g/4 oz	tomatoes, skinned, seeded and chopped	225 g/8 oz
	pinch of dried basil	
	pinch of dried oregano	
45 ml/3 tbsp	dry red wine	75 ml/5 tbsp
7.5 ml/1½ tsp	tomato purée	15 ml/1 tbsp
5 ml/1 tsp	chopped fresh parsley	10 ml/2 tsp
	salt and freshly ground black pepper	

For one

- Place the butter and onion in a bowl. Cover and microwave on HIGH for ¾ minute until soft.
- Stir in the flour, blending well. Microwave on HIGH for a further ¼ minute.
- Gradually add the tomatoes, basil, oregano, wine, tomato purée, parsley and salt and pepper to taste, blending well.
- Microwave on HIGH for 2 minutes, stirring once.
- Purée in a blender or push through a fine sieve.

For two

- Place the butter and onion in a bowl. Cover and microwave on HIGH for 1½ minutes until soft.
- Stir in the flour, blending well. Microwave on HIGH for a further ¼ minute.
- Gradually add the tomatoes, basil, oregano, wine, tomato purée, parsley and salt and pepper to taste, blending well.
- Microwave on HIGH for 3½-4 minutes, stirring once.
- Purée in a blender or push through a fine sieve.

Gravy

This is a simple gravy suitable to serve with roast meats. Use the appropriate meat stock and for extra flavour try adding a little cooked onion or a few chopped fresh herbs.

FOR ONE		FOR TWO
7.5 ml/1½ tsp	cooked meat pan juices or drippings	15 ml/1 tbsp
5-7.5 ml/1-1½ tsp	flour	10-15 ml/2-3 tsp
75 ml/5 tbsp	hot stock	150 ml/¼ pint
	salt and freshly ground black pepper	

For one ——

- Place the pan juices or drippings in a bowl with the flour, blending well. Microwave on HIGH for 1-1½ minutes until the flour turns golden.
- Gradually add the stock, blending well. Microwave on HIGH for ¾-1 minute, stirring twice until smooth and thickened. Season to taste with salt and pepper. Serve hot.

For two ——

- Place the pan juices or drippings in a bowl with the flour, blending well. Microwave on HIGH for 1½-2 minutes until the flour turns golden.
- Gradually add the stock, blending well. Microwave on HIGH for 1½-1¾ minutes, stirring twice until smooth and thickened. Season to taste with salt and pepper. Serve hot.

Speedy custard sauce

Not the 'real' egg custard sauce but just as delicious.

FOR ONE		FOR TWO
7.5 ml/1½ tsp	custard powder	15 ml/1 tbsp
7.5-15 ml/1½-3 tsp	sugar	15-30 ml/1-2 tbsp
150 ml/¼ pint	milk	300 ml/½ pint
	few drops of vanilla essence	

For one ——

- Mix the custard powder with the sugar and a little of the milk to make a smooth paste. Gradually blend in the remaining milk. Microwave on HIGH for 2-3 minutes until smooth and thick, whisking every 1 minute.
- Add a few drops of vanilla essence, blending well.

For two ——

- Mix the custard powder with the sugar and a little of the milk to make a smooth paste. Gradually blend in the remaining milk. Microwave on HIGH for 3-4 minutes until smooth and thick, whisking every 1 minute.
- Add a few drops of vanilla essence, blending well.

Apple sauce

Apple sauce is an indispensable accompaniment to roast pork, but it is also tasty with sausages and game. The commercially prepared kind is never quite like the real thing so it is well worth the effort.

FOR ONE		FOR TWO
100 g/4 oz	cooking apples, peeled, cored and sliced	225 g/8 oz
	knob of butter	
	dash of lemon juice	
2.5 ml/½ tsp	sugar	5 ml/1 tsp
5 ml/1 tsp	water	10 ml/2 tsp

For one ——

- Place the apples, butter, lemon juice, sugar and water in a bowl. Cover and microwave on HIGH for 2-3 minutes until the apple is soft and tender.
- Beat with a wooden spoon until smooth.

For two ——

- Place the apples, butter, lemon juice, sugar and water in a bowl. Cover and microwave on HIGH for 4-5 minutes until the apple is soft and tender.
- Beat with a wooden spoon until smooth.

Garlic butter

Addicts to this butter find it irresistible with French bread, on succulent steaks, with vegetables, seafood and sandwiches. Wrap any unused garlic butter and store in the refrigerator for up to 1 week.

FOR ONE		FOR TWO
25 g/1 oz	butter	50 g/2 oz
½	garlic clove, peeled and crushed	1
	dash of Dijon mustard	
	salt and freshly ground black pepper	

For one

* Place the butter in a bowl and microwave on HIGH for 5-10 seconds to soften.
* Add the garlic, mustard and salt and pepper to taste and beat until smooth and blended. Cover and chill until required.

For two

* Place the butter in a bowl and microwave on HIGH for 10-15 seconds to soften.
* Add the garlic, mustard and salt and pepper to taste and beat until smooth and blended. Cover and chill until required.

Devilled chilli butter

Hot and spicy, ideal with shellfish, pork, and mackerel.

FOR ONE		FOR TWO
25 g/1 oz	butter	50 g/2 oz
10 ml/2 tsp	finely chopped red pepper	15 ml/1 tbsp
1.25 ml/¼ tsp	mustard powder	2.5 ml/½ tsp
2.5 ml/½ tsp	Worcestershire sauce	5 ml/1 tsp
2.5 ml/½ tsp	lemon juice	5 ml/1 tsp
	salt and cayenne pepper	

For one

* Place the butter in a bowl and microwave for 5-10 seconds to soften.
* Add the red pepper, mustard powder, Worcestershire sauce, lemon juice and salt and cayenne pepper to taste and beat until smooth and blended. Cover and chill until required.

For two

* Place the butter in a bowl and microwave for 10-15 seconds to soften.
* Add the red pepper, mustard powder, Worcestershire sauce, lemon juice and salt and cayenne pepper to taste and beat until smooth and blended. Cover and chill until required.

Blue cheese and chive butter

This rich creamy butter is tasty on steaks, mushrooms, sandwiches and canapés.

FOR ONE		FOR TWO
25 g/1 oz	butter	50 g/2 oz
15 g/½ oz	blue Stilton or Danish Blue, mashed	25 g/1 oz
10 ml/2 tsp	snipped chives	20 ml/4 tsp
	salt and freshly ground black pepper	

For one

* Place the butter in a bowl and microwave on HIGH for 5-10 seconds to soften.
* Add the cheese, chives and salt and pepper to taste and beat until smooth and blended. Cover and chill until required.

For two

* Place the butter in a bowl and microwave on HIGH for 10-15 seconds to soften.
* Add the cheese, chives and salt and pepper to taste and beat until smooth and blended. Cover and chill until required.

161

Florimon dressing

It is essential to cook the garlic in this dressing to extract the full flavour. Use in salads or with cooked vegetables.

FOR ONE		FOR TWO
½	garlic clove, halved	1
15 ml/1 tbsp	olive or safflower oil	30 ml/2 tbsp
15 ml/1 tbsp	lemon juice	30 ml/2 tbsp
	pinch of ground paprika	
	salt	
	pinch of sugar	

For one —

* Place the garlic and oil in a bowl. Cover and microwave on HIGH for ½ minute. Leave to stand for 5 minutes.
* Remove the garlic with a slotted spoon and discard.
* Gradually beat the lemon juice into the oil to make a thick creamy vinaigrette.
* Add the paprika and salt and sugar to taste, blending well. Use at once.

For two —

* Place the garlic and oil in a bowl. Cover and microwave on HIGH for 1 minute. Leave to stand for 5 minutes.
* Remove the garlic with a slotted spoon and discard.
* Gradually beat the lemon juice into the oil to make a thick creamy vinaigrette.
* Add the paprika and salt and sugar to taste, blending well. Use at once.

Mock mayonnaise

A cooked mayonnaise style dressing thickened with set natural yogurt.

FOR ONE		FOR TWO
5 ml/1 tsp	plain flour	10 ml/2 tsp
2.5 ml/½ tsp	mustard powder	5 ml/1 tsp
20 ml/4 tsp	brown sugar	40 ml/8 tsp
50 ml/2 fl oz	water	100 ml/4 fl oz
½	egg yolk	1
10 ml/2 tsp	wine vinegar	20 ml/4 tsp
50 ml/2 fl oz	olive or safflower oil	100 ml/4 fl oz
	salt and freshly ground black pepper	
10 ml/2 tsp	snipped chives (optional)	20 ml/4 tsp
15-30 ml/1-2 tbsp	set natural yogurt	30-60 ml/2-4 tbsp

For one —

- Mix the flour with the mustard, sugar and water in a bowl, blending well. Microwave on HIGH for 2-2½ minutes, stirring three times.
- Meanwhile mix the egg yolk with the vinegar and oil, blending well. Add the mustard mixture and whisk well to blend.
- Add salt and pepper to taste and chives if liked, blending well. Allow to cool.
- Stir in the yogurt into the cold dressing just before serving.

For two —

- Mix the flour with the mustard, sugar and water in a bowl, blending well. Microwave on HIGH for 4 minutes, stirring three times.
- Meanwhile mix the egg yolk with the vinegar and oil, blending well. Add the mustard mixture and whisk well to blend.
- Add salt and pepper to taste and chives if liked, blending well. Allow to cool.
- Stir in the yogurt into the cold dressing just before serving.

DESSERTS

Glazed oranges

This is an ideal way of serving the juicy summer oranges that are cheap and plentiful from May to October. Serve with an unusual ice cream for a special occasion – almond complements their flavour admirably.

FOR ONE		FOR TWO
2	small summer oranges	4
45 ml/3 tbsp	water	90 ml/6 tbsp
75 g/3 oz	granulated sugar	175 g/6 oz

For one —

- ◆ Peel the oranges, removing the pith and membrane, slice thinly and put into a serving dish.
- ◆ Place the water and sugar in a bowl. Microwave on HIGH for 2-3 minutes until bubbly and syrupy, stirring three times.
- ◆ Pour the syrup over the oranges and leave until cold. Chill thoroughly before serving.

For two —

- ◆ Peel the oranges, removing the pith and membrane, slice thinly and put into a serving dish.
- ◆ Place the water and sugar in a bowl. Microwave on HIGH for 4-5 minutes until bubbly and syrupy, stirring three times.
- ◆ Pour the syrup over the oranges and leave until cold. Chill thoroughly before serving.

Cook's tip

Try using fruit such as peach, nectarines or grapes instead of oranges.

Red fruits salad

Fruit salads are naturally colourful and very easy to make. Use grenadine fruit syrup as the base for this delicious summer dessert.

FOR ONE		FOR TWO
25 g/1 oz	blackcurrants, topped and tailed	50 g/2 oz
20 ml/4 tsp	grenadine fruit syrup	40 ml/8 tsp
20 ml/4 tsp	water	40 ml/8 tsp
25 g/1 oz	raspberries, hulled	50 g/2 oz
25 g/1 oz	strawberries, hulled and sliced	50 g/2 oz
25 g/1 oz	cherries, halved and stoned	50 g/2 oz

For one ——

- Place the blackcurrants, grenadine fruit syrup and water in a bowl. Cover and microwave on HIGH for 1 minute, stirring once.
- Transfer to a serving bowl and stir in the raspberries, strawberries and cherries, blending well.
- Chill thoroughly before serving with single cream.

For two ——

- Place the blackcurrants, grenadine fruit syrup and water in a bowl. Cover and microwave on HIGH for 1½ minutes, stirring once.
- Transfer to a serving bowl and stir in the raspberries, strawberries and cherries, blending well.
- Chill thoroughly before serving with single cream.

Cook's tip

Try using red wine instead of the water, redcurrants instead of the blackcurrants and blackcurrant syrup instead of the grenadine syrup.

Mulled fruits with port

A delicious mixture of berry fruits and melon nestling in a port wine syrup. Use sherry as an alternative to port if preferred.

FOR ONE		FOR TWO
7.5 ml/1½ tsp	orange or lemon juice	15 ml/1 tbsp
25 ml/1 fl oz	port	50 ml/2 fl oz
	pinch of ground nutmeg	
	pinch of ground mixed spice	
2	cloves	2
7 g/¼ oz	caster sugar	15 g/½ oz
50 g/2 oz	strawberries, hulled, left whole or sliced	100 g/4 oz
50 g/2 oz	raspberries	100 g/4 oz
50 g/2 oz	melon, diced	100 g/4 oz
	mint sprigs, to decorate (optional)	

For one ——

- ◆ Place the orange or lemon juice, port, nutmeg, mixed spice, cloves and sugar in a bowl. Microwave on HIGH for 1 minute, stirring twice. Remove and discard the cloves.
- ◆ Place the strawberries, raspberries and melon in a serving bowl. Pour over the port syrup. Serve hot or cold decorated with mint sprigs.

For two ——

- ◆ Place the orange or lemon juice, port, nutmeg, mixed spice, cloves and sugar in a bowl. Microwave on HIGH for 2 minutes, stirring twice. Remove and discard the cloves.
- ◆ Place the strawberries, raspberries and melon in a serving bowl. Pour over the port syrup. Serve hot or cold decorated with mint sprigs.

Pineapple promise

One of the simplest creamy but refreshing chilled summer desserts I know. Serve on the day of making.

FOR ONE		FOR TWO
¼ x 375 g/13 oz	can crushed pineapple	½ x 375 g/13 oz
3.75 ml/¾ tsp	powdered gelatine	7.5 ml/1½ tsp
45 ml/3 tbsp	double cream	75 ml/5 tbsp
150 ml/¼ pint	cold Speedy Custard Sauce (see page 158)	300 ml/½ pint
	whipped cream and pistachio nuts, to decorate	

For one

- ◆ Drain the syrup from the crushed pineapple and mix with the gelatine. Leave for about 5 minutes until spongy then microwave on HIGH for ¼-½ minute until clear and dissolved.
- ◆ Whip the cream until it stands in soft peaks and fold into the pineapple with the custard and the gelatine mixture. Spoon into a dessert glass and chill until set.
- ◆ Decorate with swirls of whipped cream and pistachio nuts and serve with crisp dessert biscuits.

For two

- ◆ Drain the syrup from the crushed pineapple and mix with the gelatine. Leave for about 5 minutes until spongy then microwave on HIGH for ½ minute until clear and dissolved.
- ◆ Whip the cream until it stands in soft peaks and fold into the pineapple with the custard and the gelatine mixture. Spoon into a dessert glass and chill until set.
- ◆ Decorate with swirls of whipped cream and pistachio nuts and serve with crisp dessert biscuits.

Cook's tip

Substitute other favourite canned fruit for the pineapple, if preferred.

Pear délice

Pears, strawberries and chocolate make an unbeatable combination in this quickly prepared dessert.

FOR ONE		FOR TWO
1	ripe dessert pear(s)	2
5 ml/1 tsp	lemon juice	10 ml/2 tsp
2	small scoops strawberry ice cream	4
2	fresh strawberries, hulled and sliced	6
25 g/1 oz	plain chocolate	50 g/2 oz
15 g/½ oz	butter	25 g/1 oz
15 ml/1 tbsp	milk	30 ml/2 tbsp

For one ——

* Peel, halve and core the pear. Toss in the lemon juice and place in a serving dish.
* Top with the strawberry ice cream and sliced strawberries. Keep cool.
* Place the chocolate in a bowl with the butter. Microwave on HIGH for 1-1¼ minutes to melt. Add the milk and stir until smooth and glossy.
* Spoon over the pear dessert and serve at once.

For two ——

* Peel, halve and core the pears. Toss in the lemon juice and place in a serving dish.
* Top each with the strawberry ice cream and sliced strawberries. Keep cool.
* Place the chocolate in a bowl with the butter. Microwave on HIGH for 2 minutes to melt. Add the milk and stir until smooth and glossy.
* Spoon over the pear dessert and serve at once.

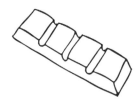

Orange mousse

Light, fluffy and refreshing orange mousse is the perfect dessert to serve after a hearty main course.

FOR ONE		FOR TWO
1	egg(s), separated	2
5 ml/1 tsp	finely grated orange rind	10 ml/2 tsp
5 ml/1 tsp	powdered gelatine	10 ml/2 tsp
30 ml/2 tbsp	water	45 ml/3 tbsp
25 ml/5 tsp	orange syrup	50 ml/2 fl oz
50 ml/2 fl oz	whipping cream	100 ml/4 fl oz
	orange slices, to decorate	

For one —

- Whisk the egg yolk and orange rind until pale and fluffy.
- Place the water in a small bowl and sprinkle over the gelatine, leave for about 5 minutes until spongy. Microwave on HIGH for ¼-½ minute until clear and dissolved.
- Fold the gelatine mixture and syrup into the egg mixture and leave until just beginning to set.
- Whisk the egg white until it stands in stiff peaks. Whip the cream until it stands in soft peaks.
- Fold the cream and egg white into the orange mixture, blending well. Spoon into a serving dish and chill until set. Decorate with orange slices.

For two —

- Whisk the egg yolks and orange rind until pale and fluffy.
- Place the water in a small bowl and sprinkle over the gelatine, leave for about 5 minutes until spongy. Microwave on HIGH for ¼-½ minute until clear and dissolved.
- Fold the gelatine mixture and syrup into the egg mixture and leave until just beginning to set.
- Whisk the egg whites until they stand in stiff peaks. Whip the cream until it stands in soft peaks.
- Fold the cream and egg whites into the orange mixture, blending well. Spoon into a serving dish and chill until set. Decorate with orange slices.

Chocolate shell mousses

The 'shell' in this recipe is a ready-made chocolate shell that can be bought at many good delicatessens or selected supermarkets. However, it isn't essential; if unavailable spoon the mousse into a small serving dish instead.

FOR ONE		FOR TWO
25 g/1 oz	plain chocolate	50 g/2 oz
	small knob of butter	
1	egg(s), separated	2
1	ready-made chocolate shell(s)	2
	grated white chocolate, to decorate	

For one ——

- Place the chocolate in a bowl and microwave on HIGH for ½-1 minute until melted. Stir in the butter, blending well.
- Add the egg yolk and beat well.
- Whisk the egg white until it stands in stiff peaks and fold into the chocolate mixture using a metal spoon. Spoon into the chocolate shell and chill until set.
- Serve chilled, sprinkled with a little grated white chocolate.

For two ——

- Place the chocolate in a bowl and microwave on HIGH for 1-1½ minutes until melted. Stir in the butter, blending well.
- Add the egg yolks and beat well.
- Whisk the egg whites until they stand in stiff peaks and fold into the chocolate mixture using a metal spoon. Spoon into the chocolate shells and chill until set.
- Serve chilled, sprinkled with a little grated white chocolate.

Bananas rhumba

A recipe from Barbados where rum is an everyday and essential ingredient. Serve with cream or ice cream.

FOR ONE		FOR TWO
1	large, firm banana(s)	2
7.5 ml/1½ tsp	lemon juice	15 ml/1 tbsp
15 ml/1 tbsp	orange juice	30 ml/2 tbsp
7.5 ml/1½ tsp	golden syrup	15 ml/1 tbsp
15 ml/1 tbsp	dark rum	30 ml/2 tbsp
15 g/½ oz	unsalted butter	25 g/1 oz
7 g/¼ oz	flaked toasted almonds	15 g/½ oz

For one ——

* Halve the banana lengthwise and place in a shallow dish. Brush with the lemon juice.
* Mix the orange juice with the golden syrup and rum, pour over the banana and dot with the butter.
* Cover loosely and microwave on HIGH for 1-1½ minutes. Sprinkle with the almonds and serve at once.

For two ——

* Halve the bananas lengthwise and place in a shallow dish. Brush with the lemon juice.
* Mix the orange juice with the golden syrup and rum, pour over the bananas and dot with the butter.
* Cover loosely and microwave on HIGH for 2-3 minutes. Sprinkle with the almonds and serve at once.

Ice cream with chocolate sauce

There are so many unusual and exotic flavours of ice cream available today that plain vanilla can seem a trifle ordinary. Lift it into the luxury class with a little chocolate sauce and it soon surpasses the rest.

FOR ONE		FOR TWO
25 g/1 oz	plain chocolate	50 g/2 oz
15 g/½ oz	unsalted butter	25 g/1 oz
15 ml/1 tbsp	milk	30 ml/2 tbsp
2	scoops vanilla ice cream	4
	chopped nuts, to decorate	

For one

* Place the chocolate in a bowl with the butter and microwave on HIGH for 1-1¼ minutes to melt.
* Add the milk and stir until smooth and glossy.
* Place the ice cream in a serving dish and spoon over the chocolate sauce.
* Decorate with a few chopped nuts and serve at once.

For two

* Place the chocolate in a bowl with the butter and microwave on HIGH for 2 minutes to melt.
* Add the milk and stir until smooth and glossy.
* Place the ice cream in a serving dish and spoon over the chocolate sauce.
* Decorate with a few chopped nuts and serve at once.

Variations

ICE CREAM WITH BUTTERSCOTCH SAUCE

To make a butterscotch sauce to serve 2, place 20 g/¾ oz butter and 100 g/4 oz soft light brown sugar in a jug. Microwave on HIGH for 1-1¼ minutes, to melt. Stir in 75 ml/5 tbsp evaporated milk and microwave on HIGH for ½-1 minute. Stir in 10 ml/2 tsp brandy, if liked. Pour over ice cream and decorate with chopped nuts.

Raspberry sundae

Sundaes are quick, colourful and popular at all times. They are also very simple to make, all you need is ice cream, tangy fruit sauce and lashings of cream.

FOR ONE		FOR TWO
50 g/2 oz	raspberries, hulled	100 g/4 oz
15 ml/1 tbsp	grenadine fruit syrup	30 ml/2 tbsp
7 g/¼ oz	caster sugar	15 g/½ oz
2	scoops vanilla ice cream	4
7 g/¼ oz	toasted flaked almonds	15 g/½ oz
	whipped cream	

For one

* Reserve a few raspberries for decoration and place the rest in a bowl. Add the grenadine fruit syrup and sugar, blending well. Cover and microwave on HIGH for 1-1½ minutes until very soft. Push through a nylon sieve or purée in a blender and leave until cold.
* To serve, place the ice cream in a serving dish. Pour over the raspberry sauce and sprinkle with the almonds.
* Decorate with a whirl of whipped cream.

For two

* Reserve a few raspberries for decoration and place the rest in a bowl. Add the grenadine fruit syrup and sugar, blending well. Cover and microwave on HIGH for 1½-2 minutes until very soft. Push through a nylon sieve or purée in a blender and leave until cold.
* To serve, place the ice cream in a serving dish. Pour over the raspberry sauce and sprinkle with the almonds.
* Decorate with a whirl of whipped cream.

Danish rødgrød

A Danish dessert of puréed berry fruits lightly thickened with cornflour. Chill then swirl with cream just before serving for a dramatic effect.

FOR ONE		FOR TWO
100 g/4 oz	redcurrants or redcurrants and blackcurrants mixed, topped and tailed	225 g/8 oz
50 g/2 oz	raspberries, hulled	100 g/4 oz
25 g/1 oz	caster sugar	50 g/2 oz
7 g/¼ oz	cornflour	15 g/½ oz
30 ml/2 tbsp	double cream	60 ml/4 tbsp

For one

* Place the redcurrants and raspberries in a bowl with the sugar. Cover and microwave on HIGH for 1½-2 minutes until tender. Purée in a blender or push through a fine nylon sieve.
* Return to the bowl and add the cornflour blended to a smooth paste with a little cold water. Microwave on HIGH for 1-2 minutes until smooth and

thickened, stirring three times. Allow to cool, stirring occasionally, to prevent a skin from forming.

* Spoon into a serving dish and chill lightly. Swirl the cream on top to serve.

For two ——

* Place the redcurrants and raspberries in a bowl with the sugar. Cover and microwave on HIGH for 2-3 minutes until tender. Purée in a blender or push through a fine nylon sieve.
* Return to the bowl and add the cornflour blended to a smooth paste with a little cold water. Microwave on HIGH for 1½-2 minutes until smooth and thickened, stirring three times. Allow to cool, stirring occasionally, to prevent a skin from forming.
* Spoon into a serving dish and chill lightly. Swirl the cream on top to serve.

Baked pears

Pears for cooking should be firm but ripe. Choose those that have started to soften at the stem end.

FOR ONE		FOR TWO
1	firm ripe pear(s)	2
15 ml/1 tbsp	brown sugar	30 ml/2 tbsp
15 g/½ oz	unsalted butter	25 g/1 oz
	pinch of ground cinnamon or ginger	

For one ——

* Halve and core the pear. Arrange cut-side up in a small dish with the thin ends to the centre of the dish.
* Sprinkle the cut surface with the sugar, dot with the butter and dust with the chosen spice.
* Cover and microwave on HIGH for 2½-3½ minutes.
* Allow to stand, covered, for 2 minutes before serving with whipped cream if liked.

For two

- Halve and core the pears. Arrange cut-side up in a small dish with the thin ends to the centre of the dish.
- Sprinkle the cut surfaces with the sugar, dot with the butter and dust with the chosen spice.
- Cover and microwave on HIGH for 4-6½ minutes.
- Allow to stand, covered, for 2 minutes before serving with whipped cream if liked.

Layered rhubarb cream

Layers of pink-tinged rhubarb cream and buttery nutty crumbs make up this inexpensive dessert.

FOR ONE		FOR TWO
100 g/4 oz	rhubarb, trimmed and chopped	225 g/8 oz
25 g/1 oz	caster sugar	50 g/2 oz
50 ml/2 fl oz	double cream	100 ml/4 fl oz
10 ml/2 tsp	icing sugar	20 ml/4 tsp
15 g/½ oz	butter	25 g/1 oz
15 g/½ oz	soft brown sugar	25 g/1 oz
40 g/1½ oz	fresh white breadcrumbs	75 g/3 oz
15 ml/1 tbsp	chopped mixed nuts	30 ml/2 tbsp
	mint sprigs, to decorate (optional)	

For one

- Place the rhubarb in a bowl with the sugar. Cover and microwave on HIGH for 3-3½ minutes until soft, stirring once. Purée in a blender or pass through a fine sieve.
- Whip the cream with the icing sugar until it stands in soft peaks and fold into the rhubarb purée.
- Place the butter, brown sugar and breadcrumbs in a bowl. Microwave on HIGH for 1-2 minutes until crisp and golden. Leave to cool then stir in the nuts.
- To serve, layer the rhubarb cream and nutty crumbs in a dessert glass. Chill thoroughly.

For two —

- Place the rhubarb in a bowl with the sugar. Cover and microwave on HIGH for 6-7 minutes until soft, stirring once. Purée in a blender or pass through a fine sieve.
- Whip the cream with the icing sugar until it stands in soft peaks and fold into the rhubarb purée.
- Place the butter, brown sugar and breadcrumbs in a bowl. Microwave on HIGH for 1½-2 minutes until crisp and golden. Leave to cool then stir in the nuts.
- To serve, layer the rhubarb cream and nutty crumbs in a dessert glass. Chill thoroughly.

Whim Wham

Whim Wham is a rather odd sounding traditional British dessert made with cream.

FOR ONE		FOR TWO
15 g/½ oz	flaked almonds	25 g/1 oz
7 g/¼ oz	unsalted butter	15 g/½ oz
7 g/¼ oz	sugar	15 g/½ oz
2	sponge fingers	4
50 ml/2 fl oz	cider	100 ml/4 fl oz
25 ml/1 fl oz	orange juice	50 ml/2 fl oz
5 ml/1 tsp	finely grated orange rind	10 ml/2 tsp
75 ml/5 tbsp	double cream	150 ml/¼ pint

For one —

- Place the almonds and butter in a bowl and microwave on HIGH for 2½ minutes until golden. Stir in the sugar and microwave on HIGH for 2½-3 minutes until caramelised. Quickly pour onto a sheet of greaseproof paper and allow to cool.
- Break the sponge fingers into large pieces and place in the bottom of a serving dish.
- Mix the cider with the orange juice and pour over the sponge fingers. Sprinkle with half of the grated orange rind.

- Whip the cream until it stands in soft peaks and swirl over the sponge fingers. Sprinkle with the remaining grated orange rind.
- Break the caramelised almonds into pieces and sprinkle over the cream. Serve lightly chilled.

For two —

- Place the almonds and butter in a bowl and microwave on HIGH for 3-4 minutes until golden. Stir in the sugar and microwave on HIGH for 3-4 minutes until caramelised. Quickly pour onto a sheet of greaseproof paper and allow to cool.
- Break the sponge fingers into large pieces and place in the bottom of 2 serving dishes.
- Mix the cider with the orange juice and pour over the sponge fingers. Sprinkle with half of the grated orange rind.
- Whip the cream until it stands in soft peaks and swirl over the sponge fingers. Sprinkle with the remaining grated orange rind.
- Break the caramelised almonds into pieces and sprinkle over the cream. Serve lightly chilled.

Crème caramels

Creamy smooth and tantalisingly light Crème Caramels are popular desserts to serve after a hearty main course.

FOR ONE		FOR TWO
15 g/½ oz	sugar	25 g/1 oz
7.5 ml/1½ tsp	water	15 ml/1 tbsp
1	egg(s)	2
7 g/¼ oz	caster sugar	15 g/½ oz
150 ml/¼ pint	milk	300 ml/½ pint

For one —

- Place the sugar and water in a small heat-resistant bowl or jug and microwave on HIGH for 1-1½ minutes until golden brown. Pour into a large tea cup or a cocotte dish.
- Whisk the egg with the caster sugar.

- Place the milk in a jug and microwave on HIGH for 1 minute. Whisk into the egg mixture, blending well.
- Strain over the caramel and microwave on LOW for 4-5 minutes until just set.
- Allow to cool then chill until set.
- To serve, unmould onto a serving dish.

For two

- Place the sugar and water in a small heat-resistant bowl or jug and microwave on HIGH for 2-2½ minutes until golden brown. Pour into 2 large tea cups or cocottes.
- Whisk the eggs with the caster sugar.
- Place the milk in a jug and microwave on HIGH for 2 minutes. Whisk into the egg mixture, blending well.
- Strain over the caramel and microwave on LOW for 9-10 minutes until just set.
- Allow to cool then chill until set.
- To serve, unmould onto a serving dish.

Cook's tip

Crème Caramels are made easily in the microwave. Cook until just set, if overcooked the custard will be curdled and unappetising.

Apricots and Curaçao

Looking for a dessert in a hurry? Then look no further than your fruit bowl – slice apricots, peaches or nectarines into a bowl, add a dash of a compatible and favourite liqueur and you have the makings of a fine feast.

FOR ONE		FOR TWO
3	fresh apricots, peeled, stoned and sliced	6
15 ml/1 tbsp	Curaçao liqueur	30 ml/2 tbsp

For one ⸺

- Place the apricot slices in a serving dish. Cover and microwave on HIGH for 1 minute.
- Add the Curaçao and mix well to blend.
- Serve at once while still warm, with a scoop of ice cream, if liked.

For two ⸺

- Place the apricot slices in a serving dish. Cover and microwave on HIGH for 2 minutes.
- Add the Curaçao and mix well to blend.
- Serve at once while still warm, with a scoop of ice cream, if liked.

Date baked apples

Baked apples stuffed with dates and sugar make delicious eating at any time of the year.

FOR ONE		FOR TWO
1	medium cooking apple(s)	2
1	large dried date(s), stoned and chopped	2
15 ml/1 tbsp	demerara sugar	30 ml/2 tbsp
7 g/¼ oz	unsalted butter	15 g/½ oz
25 ml/1 fl oz	cider	50 ml/2 fl oz

For one ⸺

- Wash the apple and remove the core. Using a sharp knife, cut a slit around the middle of the apple to prevent the skin from bursting during cooking. Stand upright in a small dish.
- Mix the date with the sugar and use to stuff the apple. Pour the cider around the apple. Cover and microwave on HIGH for 2-3 minutes until just tender.
- Serve at once with custard or cream.

For two ⸺

- Wash the apples and remove the core. Using a sharp knife, cut a slit around the middle of the apple to prevent the skin from bursting during cooking. Stand upright in a small dish.

- Mix the dates with the sugar and use to stuff the apple. Pour the cider around the apple. Cover and microwave on HIGH for 5-6 minutes until just tender.
- Serve at once with custard or cream.

Damson compote

A soothing, warm fruit compote made with damsons, sherry, sliced oranges and sultanas. Delicious served with a swirl of soured cream or natural yogurt.

FOR ONE		FOR TWO
15 g/½ oz	sultanas	25 g/1 oz
45 ml/3 tbsp	medium dry sherry or Madeira	75 ml/5 tbsp
10 ml/2 tsp	dark brown sugar	20 ml/4 tsp
1	small orange(s), peeled, pith removed and segmented	2
1	cinnamon stick	1
75 g/3 oz	damsons, halved and stoned	175 g/6 oz

For one ——

- Place the sultanas, sherry or Madeira, sugar, any juices from preparing the orange and the cinnamon stick in a bowl. Cover and microwave on HIGH for ½ minute. Leave to cool, covered.
- Remove and discard the cinnamon stick. Add the orange slices and damsons, blending well. Cover and microwave on HIGH for 1½-2 minutes, stirring once. Leave to stand, covered, for 3 minutes.
- Serve at once with a swirl of soured cream, if liked.

For two ——

- Place the sultanas, sherry or Madeira, any juices from preparing the oranges and the cinnamon stick in a bowl. Cover and microwave on HIGH for 1 minute. Leave to cool, covered.
- Remove and discard the cinnamon stick. Add the orange slices and damsons, blending well. Cover and microwave on HIGH for 2-3 minutes, stirring once. Leave to stand, covered, for 3 minutes.
- Serve at once with a swirl of soured cream, if liked.

Orchard dried fruit salad

Almost any mixture of dried fruits can be used in this recipe – pears, apples, prunes, figs, dates, raisins or bananas.

FOR ONE		FOR TWO
100 g/4 oz	mixed dried fruits	225 g/8 oz
50 ml/2 fl oz	cold tea	100 ml/4 fl oz
50 ml/2 fl oz	water	100 ml/4 fl oz
15 ml/1 tbsp	clear honey	30 ml/2 tbsp
5 ml/1 tsp	lemon juice	10 ml/2 tsp
1	small cinnamon stick	1
2	whole cloves	2
7.5 ml/1½ tsp	brandy (optional)	15 ml/1 tbsp
15 g/½ oz	blanched almonds	25 g/1 oz

For one

- Mix the fruits with the tea, water, honey, lemon juice, cinnamon stick and cloves in a bowl. Cover and leave to soak for 2 hours.
- Microwave on HIGH for 4-5 minutes until the fruit is tender, stirring twice.
- Remove and discard the cinnamon stick and cloves. Add the brandy, if liked and the almonds, blending well. Re-cover and leave to stand for 5 minutes.
- Serve warm or cold with cream, yogurt or ice cream.

For two

- Mix the fruits with the tea, water, honey, lemon juice, cinnamon stick and cloves in a bowl. Cover and leave to soak for 2 hours.
- Microwave on HIGH for 8-10 minutes until the fruit is tender, stirring twice.
- Remove and discard the cinnamon stick and cloves. Add the brandy, if liked and the almonds, blending well. Re-cover and leave to stand for 5 minutes.
- Serve warm or cold with cream, yogurt or ice cream.

Simple lemon cheesecake

A creamy smooth cheesecake made quickly and effectively with custard, cream cheese and jelly.

FOR ONE		FOR TWO
15 g/½ oz	butter	25 g/1 oz
2	digestive biscuits, crushed	4
3	lemon jelly cubes	6
5 ml/1 tsp	finely grated lemon rind	10 ml/2 tsp
10 ml/2 tsp	lemon juice	20 ml/4 tsp
30 ml/2 tbsp	water	60 ml/4 tbsp
50 g/2 oz	cream cheese	100 g/4 oz
150 ml/¼ pint	Speedy Custard Sauce (see page 158)	300 ml/½ pint
	whipped cream and fresh fruit, to decorate (optional)	

For one —

- Place the butter in a bowl and microwave on HIGH for ¼-½ minute to melt. Stir in the biscuit crumbs, coating well.
- Use to line the base of a 15 cm/5 inch diameter small deep loose-bottomed tartlet tin. Chill until set.
- Place the jelly cubes, lemon rind, lemon juice and water in a bowl. Microwave on HIGH for 1 minute to dissolve, stirring once.
- Beat the cheese until soft then stir in the jelly mixture and the custard, blending well. Leave to cool until syrupy then pour over the biscuit base. Chill.
- To serve, remove from the tin and decorate with cream and fruit, if liked.

For two —

- Place the butter in a bowl and microwave on HIGH for ½ minute to melt. Stir in the biscuit crumbs, coating well.
- Use to line the base of two 15 cm/5 inch diameter small deep loose-bottomed tartlet tins. Chill until set.
- Place the jelly cubes, lemon rind, lemon juice and water in a bowl. Microwave on HIGH for 1½ minutes to dissolve, stirring once.
- Beat the cheese until soft then stir in the jelly mixture and the custard, blending well. Leave to cool until syrupy then pour over the biscuit base. Chill.
- To serve, remove from the tins and decorate with cream and fruit, if liked.

Peach macaroons

I first tested this recipe with macaroon biscuits and was delighted with the result. Later, in a fit of extravagance, I tried using Amaretti di Saronno biscuits and adored it.

FOR ONE		FOR TWO
1	firm peach(es) (white if available), peeled, halved and stoned	2
2	macaroon or Amaretti di Saronno biscuits	4
7 g/¼ oz	flaked almonds	15 g/½ oz
7.5 ml/1½ tsp	clear honey	15 ml/1 tbsp
45 ml/3 tbsp	dry white wine	75 ml/5 tbsp

For one ——

- Place the peach halves in a shallow dish.
- Coarsely crush the biscuits and mix with the almonds. Spoon into the peach cavities and trickle over the honey.
- Spoon a little of the wine over the biscuit mixture to moisten slightly then pour the remainder around the peaches.
- Partially cover and microwave on HIGH for 1-1½ minutes. Serve hot or cold with cream, if liked.

For two ——

- Place the peach halves in a shallow dish.
- Coarsely crush the biscuits and mix with the almonds. Spoon into the peach cavities and trickle over the honey.
- Spoon a little of the wine over the biscuit mixture to moisten slightly then pour the remainder around the peaches.
- Partially cover and microwave on HIGH for 2-3 minutes. Serve hot or cold with cream, if liked.

Apple and orange crumble

A traditional oven-baked favourite made in a trice using the microwave. Brown under a preheated grill for a golden crust, if liked.

FOR ONE		FOR TWO
100 g/4 oz	peeled, cored and sliced dessert apples	225 g/8 oz
5 ml/1 tsp	finely grated orange rind	10 ml/2 tsp
25 g/1 oz	butter	50 g/2 oz
40 g/1½ oz	plain flour	75 g/3 oz
15 g/½ oz	soft brown sugar	25 g/1 oz

For one

- Place the apples in a small heatproof dish and sprinkle with the orange rind.
- Rub the butter into the flour until the mixture resembles fine breadcrumbs then stir in the sugar, blending well.
- Spoon on top of the fruit and microwave on HIGH for 3½-4 minutes until cooked. Brown under a preheated grill, if liked.

For two

- Place the apples in a small heatproof dish and sprinkle with the orange rind.
- Rub the butter into the flour until the mixture resembles fine breadcrumbs then stir in the sugar, blending well.
- Spoon on top of the fruit and microwave on HIGH for 7-8 minutes until cooked. Brown under a preheated grill, if liked.

Rice and raisin pudding

Few puddings are as popular as this creamy and comforting nursery favourite.

FOR ONE		FOR TWO
25 g/1 oz	short grain rice	50 g/2 oz
250 ml/8 fl oz	milk	475 ml/16 fl oz
50 ml/2 fl oz	evaporated milk	100 ml/4 fl oz
15 g/½ oz	brown sugar	25 g/1 oz
25 g/1 oz	raisins	50 g/2 oz
	pinch of ground nutmeg	

For one ——

- Place the rice, milk, evaporated milk and sugar in a bowl. Cover and microwave on HIGH for 3 minutes, stirring once.
- Reduce the power setting to MEDIUM and microwave for a further 18 minutes, stirring once halfway through the cooking time.
- Stir in the raisins and nutmeg, blending well. Cover and leave to stand for 5 minutes before serving.

For two ——

- Place the rice, milk, evaporated milk and sugar in a bowl. Cover and microwave on HIGH for 5 minutes, stirring once.
- Reduce the power setting to MEDIUM and microwave for a further 27 minutes, stirring once halfway through the cooking time.
- Stir in the raisins and nutmeg, blending well. Cover and leave to stand for 5 minutes before serving.

Storecupboard standby

A storecupboard favourite made simply in the microwave, try adding chopped nuts or dried fruit such as apricots or dates as a healthy variation.

Red top castle puddings

Red top castle puddings are individual sponge puddings that are cooked in small cups or glass dariole pudding moulds and topped with raspberry or strawberry jam.

FOR ONE		FOR TWO
15 ml/1 tbsp	raspberry or strawberry jam	30 ml/2 tbsp
25 g/1 oz	butter	50 g/2 oz
25 g/1 oz	caster sugar	50 g/2 oz
	few drops vanilla essence	
½	egg, beaten	1
25 g/1 oz	self-raising flour	50 g/2 oz
5 ml/1 tsp	milk	10-15 ml/2-3 tsp

For one

- Place the jam in the base of a greased cup or glass dariole mould.
- Cream the butter and sugar until light and fluffy. Add the vanilla essence and egg, beating well to blend. Fold in the flour and milk.
- Spoon into the cup or mould over the jam. Microwave on HIGH for 1½-2 minutes. Leave to stand for 5 minutes before turning out onto a plate to serve. Serve hot with custard, if liked.

For two

- Place the jam in the base of two greased cups or glass dariole moulds.
- Cream the butter and sugar until light and fluffy. Add the vanilla essence and egg, beating well to blend. Fold in the flour and milk.
- Spoon into the cups or moulds over the jam. Microwave on HIGH for 3-4 minutes. Leave to stand for 5 minutes before turning out onto a plate to serve. Serve hot with custard, if liked.

Bread and butter pudding

A scrumptious pudding to make with leftover bread. Place under a preheated grill to crisp and brown before serving.

FOR ONE		FOR TWO
2	slices white bread, crusts removed	4
25 g/1 oz	butter	50 g/2 oz
20 g/¾ oz	sultanas	40 g/1½ oz
1	egg(s), beaten	2
15 g/½ oz	caster sugar	25 g/1 oz
150 ml/¼ pint	milk	300 ml/½ pint
	few drops of vanilla essence	
	ground nutmeg	

For one

- Lightly grease a 450 ml/¾ pint pie dish.
- Spread the bread slices with the butter and cut into triangles. Layer in the pie dish with the sultanas.
- Beat the eggs with the sugar, blending well. Place the milk in a jug and microwave on HIGH for ¼-½ minute until hot. Pour into the egg mixture

with a little vanilla essence to taste. Pour over the bread slices and microwave on HIGH, uncovered, for 1½ minutes.

- Press the bread down into the egg mixture and leave to stand for 3 minutes. Microwave on HIGH uncovered, for a further 2 minutes. Leave to stand for 10 minutes.
- Microwave on HIGH, uncovered, for a further 1-2 minutes until the custard has set.
- Sprinkle with nutmeg. Serve hot or warm.

For two

- Lightly grease a 900 ml/1½ pint pie dish.
- Spread the bread slices with the butter and cut into triangles. Layer in the pie dish with the sultanas.
- Beat the eggs with the sugar, blending well. Place the milk in a jug and microwave on HIGH for ½-¾ minute until hot. Pour into the egg mixture with a little vanilla essence to taste. Pour over the bread slices and microwave on HIGH, uncovered, for 1½ minutes.
- Press the bread down into the egg mixture and leave to stand for 3 minutes. Microwave on HIGH uncovered, for a further 3½ minutes. Leave to stand for 10 minutes.
- Microwave on HIGH, uncovered, for a further 2-3 minutes until the custard has set.
- Sprinkle with nutmeg. Serve hot or warm.

Lemon zabaglione

Light, airy and sophisticated – serve with langue de chat biscuits or sponge fingers.

FOR ONE		FOR TWO
1	egg yolk(s)	2
15 ml/1 tbsp	caster sugar	30 ml/2 tbsp
30 ml/2 tbsp	Marsala or sweet sherry	60 ml/4 tbsp
2.5 ml/½ tsp	finely grated lemon rind	5 ml/1 tsp

For one

* Using an electric beater whisk the egg yolk and sugar until thick and creamy.
* Place the Marsala or sherry and lemon rind in a small bowl and microwave on HIGH for ¼-½ minute until just boiling.
* Pour onto the egg mixture and whisk until thickened. Microwave on LOW for ½ minute then whisk for about 3-4 minutes until thick and frothy.

For two

* Using an electric beater whisk the egg yolk and sugar until thick and creamy.
* Place the Marsala or sherry and lemon rind in a small bowl and microwave on HIGH for ¼-½ minute until just boiling.
* Pour onto the egg mixture and whisk until thickened. Microwave on LOW for ½-1 minute then whisk for about 3-4 minutes until thick and frothy.

Blackcurrant and kiwi kissel

A refreshing light dessert of puréed blackcurrants cooked in honey and topped with paper thin slices of kiwi fruit.

FOR ONE		FOR TWO
100 g/4 oz	blackcurrants, topped and tailed	225 g/8 oz
15 ml/1 tbsp	clear honey	30 ml/2 tbsp
5 ml/1 tsp	lemon juice	10 ml/2 tsp
60 ml/4 tbsp	water	120 ml/8 tbsp
7 g/¼ oz	wholemeal flour	15 g/½ oz
½	kiwi fruit, peeled and very thinly sliced	1

For one

* Place the blackcurrants, honey, lemon juice and water in a bowl. Cover and microwave on HIGH for 2-3 minutes until soft. Purée in a blender then sieve to remove any seeds and skin.
* Place the flour in a bowl and mix to a smooth paste with a little of the blackcurrant purée. Gradually add the remaining purée and microwave on HIGH for 1-2 minutes until thickened, stirring every ½ minute to keep the dessert smooth.
* Spoon into a serving dish and float the kiwi slices on top. Serve with whipped cream.

For two

- Place the blackcurrants, honey, lemon juice and water in a bowl. Cover and microwave on HIGH for 3-4 minutes until soft. Purée in a blender then sieve to remove any seeds and skin.
- Place the flour in a bowl and mix to a smooth paste with a little of the blackcurrant purée. Gradually add the remaining purée and microwave on HIGH for 1½-2 minutes until thickened, stirring every ½ minute to keep the dessert smooth.
- Spoon into a serving dish and float the kiwi slices on top. Serve with whipped cream.

Nutty chocolate mug cake

I have been introduced to several 'mug cakes' over the years and this chocolate one, made with cocoa but also nut butter or spread, is a favourite. We tend to serve with a spoonful of whipped cream on top but it's also fabulous with a small scoop of ice cream.

FOR ONE		FOR TWO
30 ml/2 tbsp	oil	60 ml/4 tbsp
1	small egg(s)	2
45 ml/3 tbsp	milk	90 ml/6 tbsp
30 ml/2 tbsp	chocolate or chocolate and nut butter	60 ml/4 tbsp
	pinch of salt	
30 ml/2 tbsp	plain flour	60 ml/4 tbsp
2.5 ml/½ tsp	baking powder	5 ml/1 tsp
45 ml/3 tbsp	unsweetened cocoa powder	90 ml/6 tbsp
15 ml/1 tbsp	ground almonds	30 ml/2 tbsp
15 ml/1 tbsp	caster sugar	30 ml/2 tbsp
1	small square(s) eating chocolate, broken into small pieces	2

For one

- Mix the oil with the egg, milk, butter and salt in a 300 ml/½ pint heatproof mug until well blended.
- Stir in the flour, baking powder, cocoa powder, almonds, caster sugar and chocolate pieces and mix very well.

- Microwave, on a plate (to catch any overspill), uncovered, on HIGH for 1½-2 minutes (depending upon whether you like your finished cake to be gooey or more cooked). Leave to stand for 2 minutes before serving warm.

For two ———

- Mix the oil with the eggs, milk, butter and salt in a bowl, until well blended.
- Stir in the flour, baking powder, cocoa powder, almonds, caster sugar and chocolate pieces and mix very well. Divide between two 300 ml/½ pint heatproof mugs.
- Microwave, individually, each on a plate (to catch any overspill), uncovered, on HIGH for 1½-2 minutes (depending upon whether you like your finished cake to be gooey or more cooked). Repeat with the second mug. Leave both to stand for 2 minutes before serving warm.

INDEX